LIVING

THE AMERICAN DREAM

BOOK ONE

The Mark and Sue Neumann Story
A Legacy of Faith, Family, and Love of Country
for our Children and the Future

"With a strong faith, each other, and hard work
most anything is possible
in this great nation that we live in."
—Mark Neumann

All Scripture, unless other marked, is from the Holy Bible, New International Version®, NIV® Copyright ©1973, 1978, 1984, 2011 by Biblica, Inc.® Used by permission. All rights reserved worldwide. Scripture is also taken from the Holy Bible, King James Version.

Much of this narrative is "as told to" Lisa J. Lickel.

Published by
HenschelHAUS Publishing, Inc.
www.henschelHAUSbooks.com
Milwaukee, Wisconsin

ISBN: 978-1-59598-850-8
E-ISBN: 978-1-59598-851-5
LCCN: 2021938321

Front cover photo: Mark and Sue Neumann on their wedding day, August 18, 1973.
Back cover photo: The Neumann family, Christmas 1983.

Yet you, Lord, are our Father.
We are the clay, you are the potter;
we are all the work of your hand.

—Isaiah 64:8

.

TABLE OF CONTENTS

PART TWO

PREFACE

This is the story of Mark and Sue Neumann. This is the story of living the American Dream. This book was written with the hope that it will inspire others to rely on their faith in God and to pursue their dreams in this, the greatest nation in God's creation.

Mark and Sue met in a fourth-grade Sunday school class. Their "puppy love" developed into full-fledged love and respect for one another. They married at a young age, a marriage that would last a lifetime.

Starting their lives together with nothing except their faith in God and each other, they built a strong family and eventually grew a very successful business that started in the basement of their home.

A life lived frugally and with self-sacrifice, with many hours of hard work, allowed them—by the grace of God—to build a successful business from which they would eventually walk away from, out of love for their country.

Faith, family, and love of country led to a life exemplifying the American Dream. This opportunity remains available in America today for those willing to rely on their faith in God and to put in the effort necessary to make it happen.

This is Book One of a three-book series. It takes the lives of Mark and Sue from early childhood through about age forty, when they set their lives aside in an attempt to help their country.

Book Two covers the years Mark spent in Congress and Book Three provides insights into their life after Congress.

PART ONE

Grounded in Faith and Family

Born and Raised in Wisconsin

Both Sue's family, the Links, and Mark's family, the Neumanns, have made southeastern and south-central Wisconsin home for generations. Like other families, their great-grandparents emigrated from Europe. They share a similar background in that both families had been involved in dairy farming. Certainly their life choices and values trickled down and had a significant influence on Sue and Mark.

Sue's maternal great-grandparents, Jacob Petry and Elisabeth Weber Petry, emigrated from Germany; her grandparents, Magdalene Petry Henning and Bernhardt Robert Henning ("Ben"), lived in Milwaukee until 1933 when they traded the new house for a farm in East Troy, Wisconsin. The city house they built was assessed taxes they could no longer afford during the era of the Great Depression, but they could take on the dairy farm with the help of a Federal Housing Administration loan.

Sue's mom, Beverly Jean Henning, the fourth of five children, was born in 1929 in the city of Milwaukee and recalled that after moving away, she wanted to go "home" until she adjusted to life in the country.

In a story echoed in the next generation, Sue's dad, Joseph, who was a friend of Beverly's older

Sue's maternal grandmother and grandfather, Magdalene Petry Henning and Bernhardt Robert Henning ("Ben").

brother Bud, met Beverly for the first time when she was just nine years old. They began dating seriously ten years later. After high school graduation, Beverly received her nursing degree from Milwaukee Hospital School of Nursing in 1950 and worked in the surgery department of the former Lakeland Hospital in Elkhorn.

"Mom always liked nursing. She liked the surgical med floor because she could take care of people, make them better, and they would get well and go home," Sue said. It was better than other departments where people might not get better. Sue chose to work in the medical field too.

Sue's father, Joseph Elmer Link, born in 1923, was six years older than Beverly and sixth of eight children born to Clara Hoerres Link and Joseph Albert Link. Joseph and Clara lived just west of the city of Milwaukee in New Berlin until sometime around 1933, when the family moved to rural East Troy to farm.

Joseph ("Jack") graduated from East Troy High School in

1942 and became a welder, then was drafted and served three years in the Navy, escorting supplies to Belfast, Ireland for D-Day, June 6, 1944, and to the Pacific front in the Philippines on V-J Day

Sue's paternal grandparents, Clara Hoerres Link and Joseph Albert Link.

on August 15, 1945. He served on various fronts and in officer training and supply positions until he was released from service in May 1946. After spending time in shop jobs in and around Milwaukee, Joseph decided to farm. Joseph and Beverly married October 6, 1951 and continued to operate the dairy farm where Sue later grew up, eventually purchasing it. Beverly remained living on the farm long after Sue's father passed away on August 23, 2007. Beverly joined our Lord as this book was being written on April 8, 2017.

Unusually peaceable for any era, Joseph remained Catholic, while Beverly kept her Lutheran faith. The couple agreed to raise the children as Beverly desired in the Lutheran faith.

Sue was born at Lakeland Hospital in Elkhorn, Wisconsin on August 30, 1954, the third of five children: Jeffrey, Joseph Jr., Sue Anne, David, and Alan. She was baptized at St. Paul's Lutheran Church in East Troy on September 26, 1954 by Pastor E.H. Semenske, and her sponsors were her grandparents, Mr. and Mrs. Ben Henning.

* * * * *

Sue's parents, Jack and Bev Link, on their wedding day, October 6, 1951.

Sue's baby picture
(approx. 2 months)

Sue's young family photo, 1966. Back row (L to R): David, Joe Jr., Jeff, Dad Link. Front row (L to R): Alan, Sue, Mom Link.

Mark's family has a remarkably similar background to Sue's. His maternal grandparents, Anton Karrels and Barbara Watry, married just before the start of World War I and, after moving about eastern Wisconsin and Michigan, settled on a dairy farm near Eagle in south-central Wisconsin. Mark's mother, Barbara Stella Jane, known as Stella, was the youngest of eight children. In 1937, the family moved to a dairy farm near Mukwonago. Stella was in eighth grade when she met Kurt Neumann, who was a year ahead of her at Mukwonago High School. Unlike Sue's parents, religion became a point of controversy when Stella, raised Catholic, decided at age eighteen to convert to Lutheran for her beau, Kurt. Stella was locked in her bedroom when she told the family, and literally had to climb out the window and down a ladder to elope.

The decision caused decades of estrangement with Stella's family, so she happily joined the Neumanns. Although she did not see her parents for many years, she remained in touch on a limited basis with her siblings.

Ken Neumann, Mark's younger brother, is working with his mother on her memoir. In *My Life Story* a section called "Life Lessons From My Early Years" frames the life view she instilled in her children.

> "*A strong work ethic will serve you well all your days. Live within your means and appreciate what you have.*
> *Have a strong sense of your values and priorities and honor them always: God is first in my heart and home; my spouse and myself are second; my children, grandchildren, and family are third; my profession and social life are fourth.*"

Mark feels the same way, though in his view, he says *commitment, or love of country* comes even before profession and social values.

Mark's paternal grandparents were also born in the United States of emigrant parents. George and Hilda (Blauert) Neumann married in the fall of 1929 in New Ulm, Minnesota, where Hilda's father had been a teacher in a Lutheran school. The Lutheran faith has long been a part of the family and vital to the present. George and Hilda moved to Mukwonago, Wisconsin, where they lived next door to St. John's Lutheran Church. George worked for Northwest Telephone Company and they raised their two sons, Kurt Bernard, born in 1930, and Paul, born in 1933.

A positive work ethic has been handed down through the generations. Mark's mother Stella emphasizes in her memoir Kurt's hard work even during his high school years, not only in school but also delivering newspapers and performing various farm-related jobs. Respect for the land and nature was instilled in the two Neumann boys and became a life-long value woven into Mark's business.

George and Hilda (Blauert) Neumann, Mark's paternal grandparents.

Stella and Kurt married September 30, 1950, and lived with Kurt's parents in Mukwonago. Kurt graduated from Milwaukee School of Engineering in 1954 with a degree in electrical engineering and went to work for Wisconsin Power and Light while continuing to study for a graduate degree. Stella worked as a switchboard operator at Northwest Telephone Company, with Hilda helping care for the growing family. Kurt initially took a job in Rockford, Illinois with SunStrand Aviation, but shortly after, in 1955, began working in Milwaukee at Delco, a division of General Motors (GM).

The family returned to live in Mukwonago near Kurt's parents. In 1957, GM built a new Delco facility in Oak Creek, Wisconsin. The space race was on, and Kurt was part of the team that worked on the gyro guidance system designed initially for military missiles, then for the space rockets that traveled to the moon.

Mark William was born February 27, 1954, at Waukesha Memorial Hospital while the family lived in Mukwonago, Waukesha County. He was the second of five siblings—

Mark's parents, Kurt and Stella Neumann, on their wedding day. September 30, 1950.

three boys and two girls—Dave, Mark, Connie, Ken, and Kathy. Mark was baptized at St. John's Lutheran Church on March 14, 1954 by Pastor L.G. Lehmann. His sponsors were Donna Ludke and Dean Evel.

The family lived in Mukwonago until 1963 when Kurt and Stella bought a fixer-upper home on Lake Beulah, about five miles west, near East Troy. Many of Mark's childhood memories from this time stem from the years spent remodeling and fixing up this home, formerly the servant's house and six-car garage built on a large estate, as well as planting thousands of trees, mostly pine seedlings. Perhaps his eventual interest in property development, home sales, and building rose from this early experience; certainly his love of living on water, shared by his future wife Sue, came from this time of life.

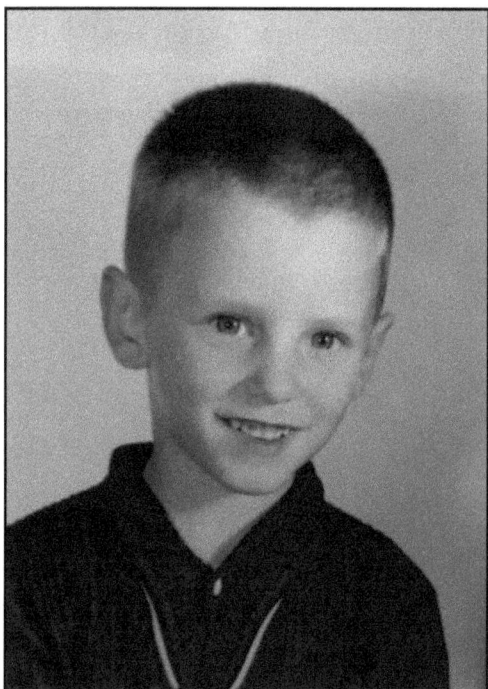

Mark (approx. age 5)

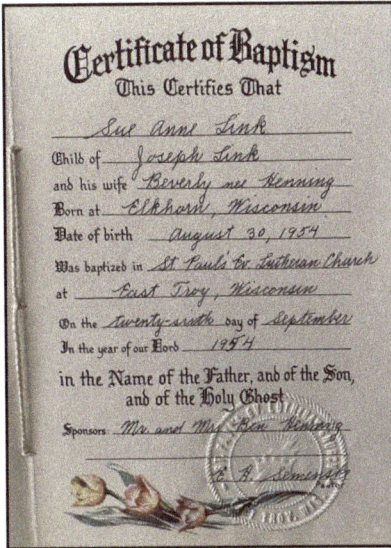

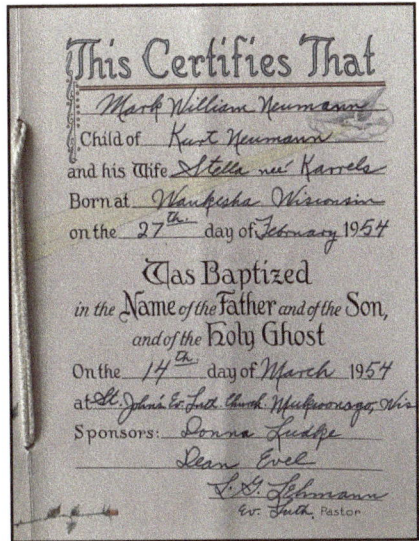

Sue and Mark's baptismal certificates.

BEFORE MARK AND SUE MET—GROWING-UP YEARS
1954-1963

Mark's early memories are of living two blocks away from his grandparents, George and Hilda, in Mukwonago next to St. John's Lutheran Church. "I would walk to Grandma's house. She would sit me on a pillow and call me 'King for the day'," he said. Mark's mother recalls Grandpa picking Mark up in the telephone company truck and taking him home. The family moved in with Grandpa in 1958 after Hilda had a heart attack and joined the Lord when Mark was barely four. "Joined the Lord" is the family's preferred phrase in reference to the death of a loved one in good relationship with God.

Later, Mark and his brother walked two blocks to Clarendon Elementary School in Mukwonago, which Mark attended from kindergarten to fourth grade.

"There was a wonderful elderly woman across the street we called Grandma Houston," Mark recalled. "I will always remember her flowers and how she worked to fill in for my missing Grandma."

Grandpa Neumann with Mark and siblings. From L to R: Ken, Mark, Kathy, Grandpa, Dave, Connie.

He has many fine memories of his grandfather, including helping shovel coal into the basement through a small window to fuel the coal-burning furnace.

"Grandpa served our country in World War I. We still have his uniform. After he joined our Lord, we found notes, and particularly meaningful were his notes on how he felt while in the trenches in Germany. He quoted Psalm 91 as his comfort while watching his friends succumb to fire and the mustard gases that filled the trenches."

Excerpts from Psalm 91

I will say of the Lord, He is my refuge and my fortress: my God; in him will I trust. <u>Surely he will save you from</u> the fowler's snare and from <u>deadly pestilence.</u> He will cover you with his feathers and under His wings you will find refuge; His faithfulness will be your shield and rampart. <u>You will not fear the terror of the night,</u> nor the arrow that flies by day...

<u>A thousand may fall at your side, ten thousand at your right hand, but it will not come near you</u>...

If you say the Lord is my refuge and make the Most High your dwelling, no harm will overtake you, <u>no disaster will come near your tent. For He will command His angels concerning you</u> in all your ways; they will lift you up in their hands...

"Because He loves me," says the Lord, "<u>I will rescue him; I will protect him,</u> for he acknowledges my name ...

I will be with him in trouble. I will deliver him and honor him. With long life I will satisfy him and show him my salvation.

"I encourage everyone to carefully read about the era," Mark said, "and picture the setting in Germany, in a trench as the mustard gas floated in, and knowing that if you raised your head for air, you would be shot. Then to appreciate what these fine folks did for us, to give us our America."

Mark's elementary school records show him to have been a fine scholar, earning As and Bs, with an occasional surprising C showing up for a quarter reporting period. His first-grade teacher was Ardith Wilcox, who noted he was absent for five days but never tardy. He grew one inch that year, 1960-61, and gained six pounds. Such physical records are no longer kept in public schools. His report cards showed an S for Satisfactory in all areas. His second grade teacher was Mildred Beltz, who awarded him an S+ in music. Arma Pratt was his third-grade teacher who gave him an "O for Outstanding" in "variety of interests," "accepts responsibility," and "exhibits resourcefulness."

Other memories Mark shared of living in Mukwonago seem to center around injuries. Not surprising, children played at the nearby schoolyard in the summers. "I had a baseball bat in my hands," Mark recalled. "Someone was hitting golf balls in the same field. One was coming my way and I decided to hit it back to him, only it hit me square in the back of my head. I still have a lump there to this day."

Another incident happened when Mark was holding the ladder for his dad. Kurt was trimming a tree when a large branch he was working on gave way unexpectedly. "It fell, knocked my

Mark's grade school picture.
(about 9 years old)

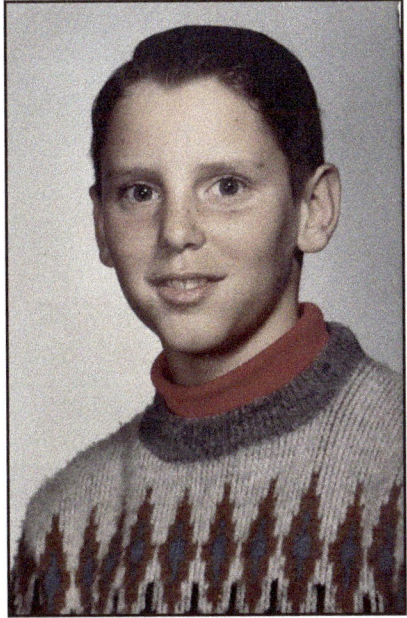

dad down, and landed squarely on me. I had a broken collarbone and needed stitches on the back of my head. Dad put me in the station wagon and drove me into town. I will never forget the doctor's office, which back then was more like a room in a house, not the emergency rooms of today."

Mark's grandfather joined the Lord in 1961. The next summer, Mark's mother went back to work, getting a job in the accounting department at AC Delco where Kurt worked as an electrical engineer. Stella's nieces babysat in the summer, and later, a family friend took care of the kids during the school year.

Both Stella and Kurt worked in Oak Creek, commuting together from Lake Beulah, thirty miles, or about an hour's drive one way even before the freeway was built, leaving home before seven a.m. and returning about six. Stella eventually became an executive assistant as her career advanced while Mark's dad worked on the space rocket guidance system project. To keep the home fires burning, the kids—typically the girls, Connie and Kathy—would warm up meals, except for Fridays, which were fried chicken and fish nights. The boys washed the dishes afterward.

Meal times were important, scheduled so that all sat together as a family. Prayer and conversation were important, and the children stayed at the table until all were finished eating and said the closing prayer. Conversation among family members was a value Mark absorbed and made a priority later while raising his and Sue's children, though typically during commutes and phone calls instead of mealtimes.

The Neumanns joined St. Paul's Lutheran Church in East Troy after the move west to Lake Beulah. The boys were in Lutheran Pioneers (more about this later), while Stella helped with Christmas pageants and the youth group. Life was busy and full.

* * * * *

Mark's family picture (1966): Back row (L to R): Connie, Mark, Mark's dad Kurt, Ken; Front row (L to R): Dave, Kathy, Mark's mom Stella.

Sue had a very traditional home life, living in the same house her whole life, the third generation of the family to live there. Mark has always held Sue's parents in high regard, sharing his opinion that her father, Joseph, was a brilliant dairy farmer and World War II veteran. Her mom, Beverly, became a homemaker once the children arrived. Beverly and Joseph's marriage of mixed faiths did not cause the tension and shunning that occurred in Mark's mother's family.

"We did not miss church," Sue said. "We went every Sunday. Dad would go to Mass (at St. Peter's Catholic Church in East Troy), and Mom took us to St. Paul's Lutheran Church (in East Troy)."

Sue remembered summer swimming lessons at nearby Booth Lake, for which a bus picked up the kids at the end of the very long driveway to the farmhouse.

If Sue's mother was considered traditional in her role as a stay-at-home mom, her dad was even more so. "I was the only girl with four brothers," Sue shared. "My dad said he didn't want me, the only daughter, to work in the barn with the dairy cows. I was to stay in the house, helping Mom with the cleaning and cooking. But I wanted to work

Sue, age 2.

in the barn too. One day I traded work with my brother Joe for a day. He stayed in the house and helped Mom, and I went out and cleaned the barn. We decided after that day we were each more suited to our regular jobs."

Sue often went with her brothers, bucket in hand, through the cornfields and pick berries which they brought home to be made into jams and other goodies.

Kittens were born regularly in the dairy barn. "Many times the mothers would abandon the kittens and I would bring them into the back hall and nurse them until they were ready to fend for themselves." She would dress them up in baby doll clothes and feed them with a doll bottle. Mark said her tender heart never changed one bit. She took many photographs of her kittens.

The farmhouse Sue grew up in.

Because of life on the farm, the endless work with feeding and milking cows, the Links could not take time for vacations away from home. "Once a year," Sue said, "we would take a day and go to the State Fair and another day at the County Fair in Elkhorn."

Sue worked regularly in the very large farm garden helping her mom preserve fruits and vegetables to feed the large family. One chore her father would allow was helping to pick sweet corn. She would sit the back of a flatbed wagon while her dad drove the tractor to and from the field. They would then husk the harvested sweet corn for a meal or the freezer to savor later during the winter months.

Joseph butchered chickens. Apparently his daughter was not too delicate to help her mom pluck the chickens and prep them for the freezer.

Fonder memories include Friday popcorn nights. "It was a family ritual," Sue said. "We had popcorn and Kool Aid. Soda was only allowed on New Year's Eve and on sick days." Popcorn and Kool Aid nights were one of two times the kids were allowed to eat in the living room instead of at the kitchen table. "My parents were strict about eating our meals at the table," Sue recalled. The other informal meal time? Sunday Green Bay Packer football game days. "I was so excited to take my plate in the living room to watch the game."

The Link kids made regular three- to four-day visits to their nearby maternal grandparent's farm every summer where Sue would help with the gardening and baking cookies. "A real treat was going to the grocery store," Sue said. "Grandma would get whatever I wanted."

Sue's family is double bonded, as her parents and aunt and uncle married siblings. Sue can explain, but part of it meant that she and her special cousin Debbie have the same aunt/mother, uncle/father combination. Sue's mom and Debbie's mom were sisters and Sue's dad and Debbie's dad were brothers. Sue and Debbie would "switch" families for a week in the summers.

Sue attended East Troy Community Schools. The school bus would pick up the kids at the end of their long farm driveway for the trip into town. Mrs. Lackey reported that in kindergarten, Sue was absent only one day. She was given A's in classroom subjects, though she "cries when confused." Otherwise, Sue was noted as speaking clearly and well, a lifelong invaluable talent in her and her future husband's careers. "Sue is a honey—is interested in all of our school work, is alert and should not have any trouble in First Grade. Am happy to have her in my room."

Mrs. F.L. Herian, Sue's third grade teacher, gave her an A average in all the study areas, Reading, Language, Spelling, Writing, Science/Health, Music, and Phy Ed. One area of note was that Sue always excelled in choral music, evidenced by her love of singing in church choirs.

"Mom was always there when we came home from school," Sue remembered. For a while, Beverly worked as a nurse two days a week, but then stayed at home. "I had a friend in school who cried one day when she was sick and couldn't go home because neither parent was available. I remember telling my friends that my mom would come and get them and take care of them because she was a nurse."

The importance of being there for the family became a priority in Sue and Mark's lives. Both retained the family values instilled in them by their family. Faith, work ethic, and family life became their mainstay through the career ups and downs, business shifts, and public service.

School Years—Mark Meets Sue, 1963-1968

Lake Beulah

The Neumann family's move to Lake Beulah in 1963 meant the older school-aged children had to attend new schools in East Troy. A neighbor took care of youngest child, Kathy, and Mark's brother Dave, the oldest son at age eleven, was deemed caretaker of his other siblings when Mark's parents continued the work commute to Oak Creek.

Weekends and many nights became house remodeling and landscaping time. Mark still recalls the years of do-it-yourself dry walling, wiring, plumbing and making their lakefront into a nice beach. Gardening too. Stella was known for her pickles— dills, bread-and-butter sweet pickles, and relish. To the time of this writing, she still enjoyed this work and Sue helped her.

"Dad didn't talk a lot about his office work," Mark said. "My memories were mostly of construction, redoing the house morning, noon, and night."

Kurt and Stella bought what had been a servant's quarters-combination six-car garage on an estate on South Shore Drive. "My dad and mom had a vision that this servant's quarters/ garage could be converted into a beautiful lakefront home for little or no money," Mark said. "We planted many, many trees on the lake property while I was growing up," Mark said. "In the front yard, we each had our own tree and were responsible for keeping it watered."

Life changed as the family all pitched in for the six-year remodeling job. They reclaimed all the lumber, as well as literally pulling and straightening nails.

Mark shook his head and laughed. "I can't believe we even reused the nails." Mark helped out by carrying things and cleaning up—the jobs no one else wanted to do. He admitted to not being hands-on much at that time, though later worked on his own home and office-building projects.

"We built our own six-foot-square fireplace in the middle of four of the garage stalls and converted the space into a spectacular family room on the first floor," Mark recalled. It sat on a raised platform. After he and Sue started dating, they spent many hours here during their high school years, with friends, after games, prom, and other activities.

The upper part of the house was converted into living space with three bedrooms, a formal living room, kitchen and bathrooms. "The work was endless. For a time, all seven of us slept in the same bedroom, as the rest of the place was completely torn apart.

"We learned how to install stucco on the exterior. The process was a bit scary when we got to the second-floor areas."

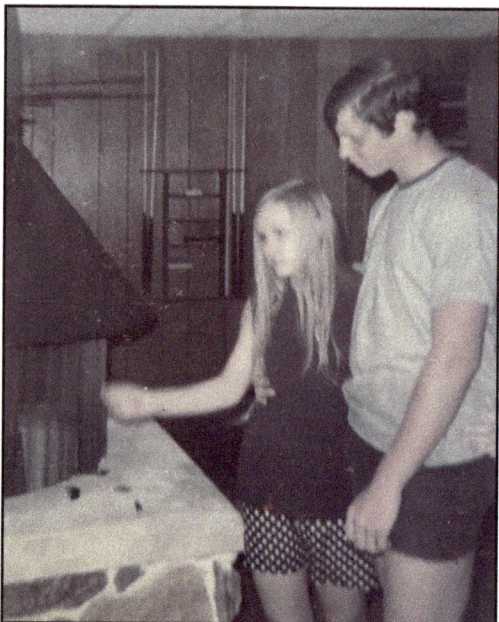

Mark and Sue at the family room fireplace.

The Lake Beulah house before remodeling.

The Lake Beulah house after remodeling.

* * * * *

Church was one activity for which there was always time. Church—and occasional picnics on the shore—were Sunday afternoon summer activities. Baloney sandwiches were a staple for the large family. "Money was always tight even with both Mom and Dad working, as they had five of us to care for."

Vacations were spent in northern Wisconsin at a cabin near St. Germaine. Also, the annual deer hunting trip to the traditional area near Florence was a big event in the family.

One particular family tradition, however, has been passed on to the fourth Neumann generation: potato chips and onion and sour cream dip during Sunday afternoon Green Bay Packer football games.

"After a while Dad decided that if we wanted a speed boat for the lake, we should earn it," Mark said. "He started paying us eighty cents an hour for some of the work, of which half went toward the purchase of the boat. Sure enough we eventually made enough money and bought a speed boat, which we all enjoyed.

"The lessons learned were to work to earn what I wanted and that a carrot makes working harder, easier. These are principles I applied later at our companies as we set goals. Once goals were achieved, we rewarded our employees, several times with trips to Maui. I remember on one trip to Maui, the wife of one of our valued employees asked what had to be done to come again. I told her, and she turned to her husband and asked him why he was not on the phone calling potential clients … we were still in Maui!"

* * * * *

The walk from the house to pick up the school bus stop was a half mile. "When you're on your own, with no protection from the weather, it can be a long walk," Mark said, even as his kids joked about the stories ("Uphill both ways, right, Dad?") later in life. Mark and his siblings attended East Troy Stewart School for the first time in the 1963-64 school year. Mark was in the fourth grade with Carolyn Perkins as his teacher, and the report cards from that time note a slight change in subjects from his former school.

The subject list on the report cards wasn't the only thing that changed. The school was a small country building with two classes in each room. "I have a very strong memory of sitting in Mrs. Perkins's fourth grade classroom and learning that President Kennedy had been shot. The world seemed turned upside down. Riots raged in Milwaukee and we lived with a constant concern they would spread to East Troy. One night, we heard what we thought were many shots being fired and I can remember my dad loading our rifles as he intended to protect us if necessary…it was a tough time in American history."

GROWING UP

Sue didn't have a clue that her life journey was about to shift when fourth grade began for her in 1963. She went right along as usual at her school with Mrs. Walsh, earning very regular As and Bs in her subject areas. But when a new boy showed up at her family church, things changed.

Mark reported officially that he and Sue were high school sweethearts who married and lived happily ever after, but the real story begins in, of all places, Sunday School at St. Paul's Lutheran Church in East Troy, Wisconsin, back in 1963.

"I sat down in Sunday school class and there was this beautiful girl with long blonde hair sitting across the table from me," Mark recalled. "I don't think she liked me very much but I knew she was special. Our family sat in front of church each week while Sue's family sat toward the back. Sue still complains

I embarrassed her as I stared at her as they walked out of church all the way from the front to the back."

"He did," Sue said. "It used to make me so uncomfortable when he'd just stare at me the whole time."

Of course the only way Sue knew Mark was staring at her was that she was watching him!

By sixth grade, Mark was a goner. He recalls distinctly her blonde hair and blue sweater which she wore to their sixth grade Christmas program at church.

Mark continued to do well in elementary academics, but Penmanship most often got him a C on his report cards; even Cs in Physical Education in fourth and fifth grades, and a C in art, though, like Sue, he earned As in music. He had the same teacher for fifth and sixth grades, Mrs. Helen Schlax, who gave him a better report for sixth grade—no Cs and an A in art.

Sue was in Mrs. G. Westphal's fifth grade class where her grades were a B average, besides the A in choir.

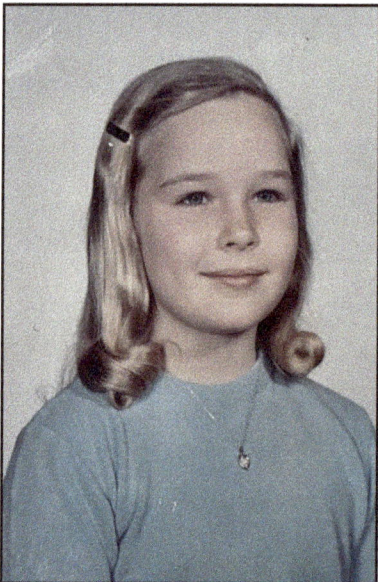

Sue's 6th-grade blue sweater.

Other life-shaping events were developed during this influential time period. Mark and Sue's incredible work ethic became deeply ingrained. Yes, the Neumann's home remodel and the Link's farm and farmhouse chores were a huge part of their lifestyle, but both their parents encouraged their children to get jobs.

"My first job, while in fourth grade, and first dollars earned," Mark said, "was to pick up a bushel basket full of hickory nuts that were sold to the Elegant Farmer," a Mukwonago business that began as a dairy farm selling surplus goods on a roadside market in the mid-1940s. The Elegant Farmer has since become a large operation selling fresh, locally grown produce, and includes a bakery and deli.

"It was great to have money in my pocket and I learned quickly that it was not going to be freely given to me, but I would be given the opportunity to earn it."

By the summer after fifth grade, Mark had the opportunity to work regular hours at an outside job. "There was a vegetable stand down the road from our house and of course, that meant growing produce for sale. My job was weeding the onions, mostly. Three hours a morning allowed me to put $1.50 in my pocket each day and I was thrilled.

"Also during this time period when the strawberries were in season I would ride my bike over to the Elegant Farmer and pick strawberries." Kids would get ten or twelve quart containers which they could fill with strawberries for ten cents a container. "I learned a hard lesson that first summer. I watched a bunch of kids from my field get fired. It turns out they were putting straw in the bottoms of the containers and filling the rest with straw- berries." In effect, cheating. Mark's eyes were opened to the fact that the world was not always the wonderful place he perceived it to be.

"After weeding the onions, there were afternoons on the lake," he said. "Fishing, swimming and, in general, enjoying being a kid on a lake. Great fun!"

Although his parents both worked long hours, family and children were priorities. There were many good times during these years, both Mark and Sue recalled. Once, when he was very sick at school, and when the school called his parent's workplace in Oak Creek, both parents came and took him to the doctor. Both Mark and Sue appreciate the value of having and being parents who made family key.

Farm life and work kept Sue close to home. "We weren't really allowed to join many activities," Sue said. "With five kids, if we all wanted to be in clubs, Mom and Dad would be running all the time, and they had to be home on the farm. I do remember a couple of friends who were in 4-H, and I would have liked to join, but knew I couldn't." Sue was content with summer activities with her farm neighbors. "We would ride bikes to each other's houses, and occasionally ride horses. We played. I was happy playing with dolls and my cousins. We were all very close, like they were my brothers and sisters."

Mark's father took him on hunting trips on public land in Florence County from the time he was thirteen. The annual gun-deer hunt has been a Wisconsin ritual for many each fall for generations. "Mom didn't want to let me go when I was twelve, as she thought I was too young." He kept his grandpa's gun, an 1899 303 lever-action Savage, and shot his first deer at age thirteen. The gun hung in Mark and Sue's living room, along with his father's Remington 308 semiautomatic rifle.

Mark vividly recalls that year he turned thirteen. "Dad told me to stay there in the stand and he'd come back later. A ten-pointer walked over a nearby hill and I shot it with Grandpa's 303 lever action rifle. He fell immediately and I ran over toward him. I forgot to eject the shell, so when the deer got up and ran, I had to eject the shell first and then shoot again. I had a whistle to call Dad, but I was so excited I forgot to use it. By the time Dad came back, I had the ten-point buck gutted on the ground at my feet."

The next year Mark shot at a doe. Five times. "It was so weird how that doe kept going," he recalled. "When I went to find it, that's when I saw the second one." He'd shot two deer instead of the one he assumed he'd had shot. "Fortunately we had two tags."

Dad, Mark, and Dave with Mark's first deer, a 10-pointer.

The following year an eight-pointer was taken from the same stand. The eight- and ten-point racks hang in Mark's office to this day and 2020 saw Mark back in the same stand with sons and grandsons hunting nearby.

* * * * *

The East Troy school system called the later elementary years "junior high." The seventh- and eighth-grade years seemed more studious, at least academically. Mark began to take French, which he continued to study for the next several years, through eleventh grade. He had his first male teacher in seventh grade, Mr. Charles Bonack, who have him As in academics and a kind Satisfactory in Penmanship. His eighth-grade teacher was Mrs. Anich, and mixed choir was one of the electives Mark chose. Both Sue and Mark recall walking to the nearby bowling alley for bowling class.

"We were in different home rooms and we both remember hoping to pass each other in the halls between classes," Mark said. Sue's sixth-grade teacher for the 1965-66 school year was Mrs. Ethel Schmidt. Sue's grades went up a notch, though down to a C in Physical Education.

A lifelong passion for sports started about this time. "Basketball was the only seventh grade sport (for boys)," Mark said. "I was six feet tall already by then and enjoyed the game greatly though I was not the best player on the team by any means.

"I continued to grow, however, and I was blessed with some athletic abilities."

Sue always wanted to be a cheerleader. She admitted never being all that good at trying out for activities. "I would get so nervous," she said. "I tried out for cheerleading in seventh grade, but didn't make the team. I was so discouraged I never tried again." She contented herself later by being Mark's number-one fan in the stands, competing for the role with Mark's mother, Stella.

* * * * *

It was during the summer of seventh grade when Mark's parents dropped him off at the Priefer farm near Mukwonago on the way to their jobs that working long hours just became a matter of habit. Mark began work at seven a.m. on the farm. "My first job every morning was to shovel out the cow manure while Ray, who had already milked by the time I got there, had breakfast. From then on, we did all the normal farm chores, from baling hay to picking stones. Mom and Dad would pick me up on their way home at a little after five each day. These were long days and included many Saturdays in haying season.

"By the second summer, I was driving the tractors. I will never forget the day I was backing up and knocked over a fifty-gallon drum of oil...all over the cow yard. I thought Ray would be really mad and I was scared how he would react. I learned a lot as he calmly helped me clean it up and explained that making unintentional mistakes is part of life."

This lesson was extremely useful later in life both in business and Washington DC politics, as was the work of shoveling manure.

CONFIRMATION

Being in the same grade at the same church meant Mark and Sue went through confirmation classes and were confirmed together. Confirmation was a two-year-long endeavor, culminating in a ceremony on May 19, 1968 at the church. Confirmands walked from the East Troy Middle School to St. Paul's Lutheran Church for the classes.

Although Mark and Sue remember this rite as an important act of faith, it was also during puberty, and, well, hormones ruled.

"One time as we walked down the railroad tracks," Mark said, "and I was up ahead with Sue's best friend, trying to make Sue jealous, and I lobbed some stones over my head in Sue's general direction. She, of course, told on me and Pastor Murphy explained that this was the behavior of a boy who liked her very much."

"The Pastor's response, 'That just means he likes you' and no punishment for Mark bothers me even now," Sue said.

They were confirmed in the Wisconsin Evangelical Lutheran Synod by the Reverend John F. Murphy. Class members received little red booklets, *Memento of my confirmation* and *The Story of my life as told in the Bible* by O. Hagedorn. Sue's booklet is filled in neatly: "My first communion" was dated May 26, 1968, along with her birth and baptism records, and her confirmation text, "Blessed are they that hear the word of God and keep it." Mark's booklet noted his birthday.

According to the keepsake church bulletin and class photograph, the others in the confirmation class include Steve Adsit, Dale Ames, Bob Frost, Sandy Jay, Robin Kiesow, Angie Omet, Debby Pontel, Dan Price, Cindy Sie, Patty Sie, and Jeff Zenke.

The class was divided by last names in alphabetical order, and while Link and Neumann would normally be able to sit next to each other in the pews, the class was divided on either side of the church aisle, six students up to Sue Link on one side, and seven students starting with Mark Neumann on the other side.

Mark and Sue's Confirmation Day, May 19, 1968.

"I was disappointed to have to sit across the aisle from Sue, again next to Sue's best friend, at our confirmation ceremony," Mark said. His eyes went soft. "Her dress was a light blue covered in lace..." Then his eyes twinkled. "That was probably the first time I really said something nice to Sue, when I told her how pretty the dress was." Sue just smiled.

Mark and Sue were members of the WELS church Young People's Society, YPS, which met monthly on Sunday evenings. It was one extracurricular activity Sue was allowed and encouraged to participate in. The group did many activities together, like hayrides, growing closer all the while. "I remember holding hands on those hayrides," Sue said.

"Really?" Mark said. "Even then?"

"Oh, yes."

Sue's blue Confirmation dress with Grandma Link and Grandpa Henning.

* * * * *

For Sue, those idyllic days of farm work were followed by time for fun at night. "There were summer dances on Wednesday nights," she said. She was just learning to sew and made her own outfits for the dances.

Mark went, too, hoping Sue would be there "and even talk to me." Sue tended to avoid him those days.

In her role as budding homemaker while growing up, Sue helped her mother with the garden, as well as with cooking and cleaning, her least favorite job. "I had to clean my brothers' room, and I couldn't understand why I had to do it when they were the ones who made the mess. The summer after sixth grade I had a rebellious streak. When Mom called out that it was time to clean, I thought, *this is the pits*. I'd had it up to here and I was not cleaning anymore. I ran away to the woods for the day. When I went back, I expected to be punished. But Mom didn't reprimand me. She just looked up and smiled and said, 'Hi, honey.' All the work had been done. I felt so guilty after that and accepted my role in the family."

One activity Sue loved was baking. Every Sunday, she would bake a special cake for the family. "I would go through the recipe books and was allowed to make anything I wanted. Mom would drive me, or later I'd drive myself into the grocery store to buy the ingredients. My dad loved fruit and whenever I'd make one that had fruit filling, he'd say how good it was."

* * * * *

Both Mark and Sue took music lessons. Mark played trombone earlier, before high school, and Sue learned to play the organ. Both of them loved vocal music, and while Sue enjoyed singing in the church choir, she was too nervous to sing in public, and tryouts in high school choir was too nerve-wracking. Mark enjoyed participating in theater during high school, often performing on stage.

There were many good times during these years, both Mark and Sue recalled.

HIGH SCHOOL SWEETHEARTS, 1968-1972

FRESHMAN YEAR, 1968-JUNE 1969

Somehow, in between the breathless non-stop schedule Mark, the "country, not-farm" kid, and his family kept, he found time to court the object of his affection, Sue, the farm kid.

For both, Sundays was church, weekdays were filled with school and afterschool activities for Mark with sports, Lutheran Pioneers, play practice, debate, forensics, ski club, work, studying. Friday evenings almost always involved some of kind of

Mark and Sue's first official date—Homecoming Dance freshman year, 1968.

sport game, and Mark was a three-sport athlete all during high school; Sue was his number-one fan. Saturdays were work or chore days.

As a fashion statement, Mark sported long sideburns in high school. "That was the thing!"

Mark and Sue attended the Homecoming Dance.

"That would be our first official date," Sue said. "It was the first time you invited me to go somewhere with you, not with the group."

"Didn't you ask me?" Mark said in jest.

Sue laughed. "No. We were old-fashioned. I wanted him to ask me—I was waiting for him to." She didn't hesitate to agree.

"Who drove us?" Mark asked. "We weren't old enough to drive back then."

"It must have been your parents," Sue said.

"Or was it Dave?" Mark said.

"Mark's older brother...no, we wouldn't have let him do that," Sue said.

Sports

Sporting activities were a learning experience. Mark earned eight high school letters—three in basketball, three in football, and two in track. "Sports were a very big part of our lives in high school, as they would be in the future," he said. While poking through their boxes of memorabilia, Mark dug out his old letterman's jacket, still jingling with medals. When urged to try it on, he hesitated, but then thrust his arms in. "Hey, it fits!" And it still looked great.

"See what you've done to us?" he teased. "This jacket goes back thirty years!"

"Honey, more like forty-five," Sue said gently.

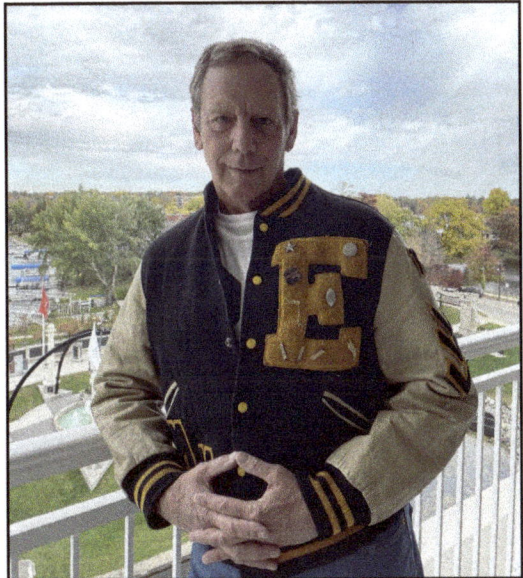

Mark's letter jacket
still fits in 2021!

BASKETBALL

Basketball was a passion from grade school on through their years of watching their children play. "Basketball was my love," Mark said. "I enjoyed football and went out for track because we wanted to be in a sport in the spring."

Sue and Mark's parents attended the games. "Though not in the same section," Sue put in. "I sat in the student section and cheered." Kurt and Sue kept track of Mark's stats on scoresheets in their own ways. "Burlington and Lake Geneva (high schools) always killed us," Mark said.

Mark attended All American Basketball Camp in Beaver Dam on August 8, 1969, where he won the Twenty-One Shooting Contest.

East Troy

East Troy Varsity

No.	Name	FG	FT	Fouls	Yr
11	Carbon, George	2222222222	1111111111	12345	11
12	Bale, Rick	2222222222	1111111111	12345	10
15	Kilpin, Mark	2222222222	111111	12345	11
21	Hiller, Jay	2222222222	1111111111	12345	11
31	Barnes, John	2222222222	1111111111	12345	12
33	Friemoth, Bob	2222222222	1111111111	12345	12
35	Piedot, Rick	2222222222	1111111111	12345	11
41	Twist, Gary	2222222222	1111111111	12345	11
43	Neumann, Mark	(23) 2	11111	12345	12
45	Hammerling, Lee	2222222	1111111111	12345	12
53	Germundson, Rob	222222	11111111	12345	12
55	Van White, Pat	2222222222	1111111111	12345	12

Coach: Jerry Schmidt

Managers: Mike Luttropp
Joe Pangburn

School Colors
Yellow & Black

Basketball score sheet kept by Mark's dad. Mark scored 23 points.

Always tall, even as a freshman, Mark played varsity basketball throughout high school. He wore #42 and was often the high scorer, earning many accolades.

"They started basketball for girls when we were seniors," Sue said, "but I wasn't much into playing sports. I was Mark's personal cheerleader from the stands."

SOPHOMORE YEAR, JUNE 1969-JUNE 1970
"THE BIG BREAKUP"

Sue's report cards from 1968, freshman year, through twelfth grade in 1972, indicate that she was tardy only one day in the fourth quarter of her senior year. Her highest marks were often in Home Economics course, with other grades bouncing around between high and low in Physical Education and one C in science in her sophomore year. "I hated dissecting frogs," she said. "I got such a bad grade in biology."

"We had a former pro football player for a teacher," Mark said. "He was huge, like six-foot–eight, and very intimidating."

Sue shivered, all these years later. "He said we had to do this dissecting, and we did it. We didn't have that class together."

Besides sharing many classes together in high school at East Troy, Mark and Sue dated and attended dances and the proms, and homecoming activities.

"Even though I wasn't much of a dancer," Mark said.

"Oh, I made you dance," Sue said.

"The slow dances—the 'Why' dances," Mark said.

Sue: "Mark's mom called them the 'why dance' dances."

Mark: "As in 'why not just stand on the floor and hug each other'."

Sue in her blue prom dress.

For the sophomore prom, which was held on May 2, 1970, with music by The Father's Children, according to the saved program, Sue wore a pretty, formal-length blue dress.

After that, was the big breakup.

"Sue gave me time off for bad behavior," Mark said with a pout. "Something about too big of an ego, as I recall."

It was an accusation of plagiarism that Sue recalls very well was about the last straw of Mark's over-the-top academic helpfulness.

One class they did have together—well, Sue put it: "I was forced to take geometry with Mark sophomore year. I distinctly remember when I would have to go up the board and prove some formula, or draw something, I was so nervous, especially knowing Mark was watching me. Geometry wasn't my thing. I was much better at Home Economics."

"She was just fine at it," Mark said.

After being intimidated in geometry class with Mark, Sue was not interested in one more symbol of inferiority in English class. "I didn't even know what plagiarism meant," Sue said, "and he told me I had copied something for my English assignment."

"I had just read it somewhere," Mark mumbled. "I'm sure I deserved whatever I got."

What he got was competition.

"We took a break—"

"Wasn't my idea—"

"It was good to go out with other people," Sue said firmly. "We learned to appreciate each other more." Their breakup lasted through the summer, fall, and after Christmas of their junior year.

* * * * *

In Track and Field, Mark was on the 1970 half-mile and mile relay teams, and the High Hurdle Shuttle relay. In field events, he took first in Discus, and fifth in High Jump.

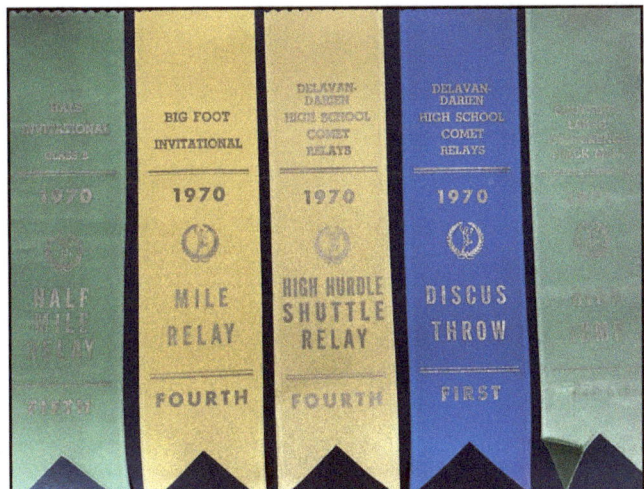

Mark's ribbons for track.

JUNIOR YEAR – JUNE 1970-JUNE 1971
"TOGETHER FOREVER"

"The year we were not together, she brought 'Greggy boy' to Homecoming and it drove me crazy," Mark said. He remained possessive of his future wife afterward and through all the years of their happy marriage, professing to be still upset about that time.

But he tried the payback route. "I found a girl from a Chicago suburb whose family had a place on Lake Beulah. I took her to Homecoming. It must have had the right effect on Sue, as we got back together again shortly thereafter."

"Shortly" was relative—the mend took about four months.

Mark and Sue went on a date for Valentine's Day, 1971. They had recently gotten class rings, and while they'd been a "couple" before their breakup, exchanging rings sealed the deal.

"I remember telling her I had to stop at home for something…my parents knew something was up when I showed up so early and left again," Mark said.

Sue thought it was a little odd, but the "something" Mark had left at home was worth the stop.

"His ring was so big," Sue said, "I had to wrap angora yarn around and around and around it so it would fit on my finger." Mark wore her ring on a chain around his neck, like other guys in the class who had steady girlfriends. Thereafter, they were inseparable, even during school activities.

"I will never forget when the girls [in Future Homemakers of America, or FHA] had bake sales," Mark said. "I would buy out everything she made. Her chocolate chip brownies were particularly deadly. I can remember buying the whole plate and then hiding them so I got them all to myself…it was not very nice in hindsight."

Mark and Sue exchanged rings their junior year in high school.

"It was embarrassing," Sue said. "He'd walk around the halls of school with the pan, saying he bought all my brownies."

But she wasn't too embarrassed to make sure everyone knew her boyfriend had the "best legs." At another FHA fund-raiser, they got the football players to stand behind a blackboard with only their bare legs showing. The students then bid on which anonymous player had the best legs. "Sue made sure I won that one, so maybe we were even," Mark quipped.

Sue gave Mark a two-by-three miniature school snapshot from 1970 with the message, "Mark, the only reason I am giving you this is because I know you wanted it. We have had many good times together which I'll never forget always some 'misinformation' which I'll try not to remember. I just hope we'll have many more good times together to come in the future. Love, always, Sue."

The "misinformation" was a deliberate act of sabotage.

"Sue's older brother Jeff and my older brother Dave were in the same class," Mark said. "They were seniors when we were sophomores."

The two cooked up a plot to break up Mark and Sue's relationship. "They'd come home with all kinds of stories about what we did at school with other people," Sue said. "When we learned what they were up to, we just disregarded their stories."

* * * * *

The fun and games of the time were interspersed with unfortunately illegal activities teens find to do.

"One night we were with a group of our 'friends,'" Mark and Sue recalled. "They pulled out drugs and asked us to join them. Thankfully, we refused."

"Looking back on this experience," Mark said, "I realize how firmly grounded in our values and beliefs we really were at that time in our lives. Later, I would lecture thousands of kids to think about how they are going to respond when challenged.

"I called it the 'Dumb Old Mark' part of virtually every talk I had with young people. The talk had three points:

1. The first was, be prepared for the test, like being tempted to try drugs

2. Second, study hard, especially your weakest subject;

3. Third, follow your dreams. Don't ever let anyone tell you that you cannot accomplish what you want.

* * * * *

Mark was inducted into the National Honor Society, Minerva Chapter, at East Troy High School on November 9, 1970. A ceremony was held November 16, 1970 at 7:30 p.m.

In basketball, Mark made Second Team All Conference under coach Jerry Kennealy. Mark was often the high scorer. His best game was most likely the one on December 1, 1970 against Elkhorn, during which he scored 22 points. In the final game of the season, he scored 18 points in a painful loss to Walworth.

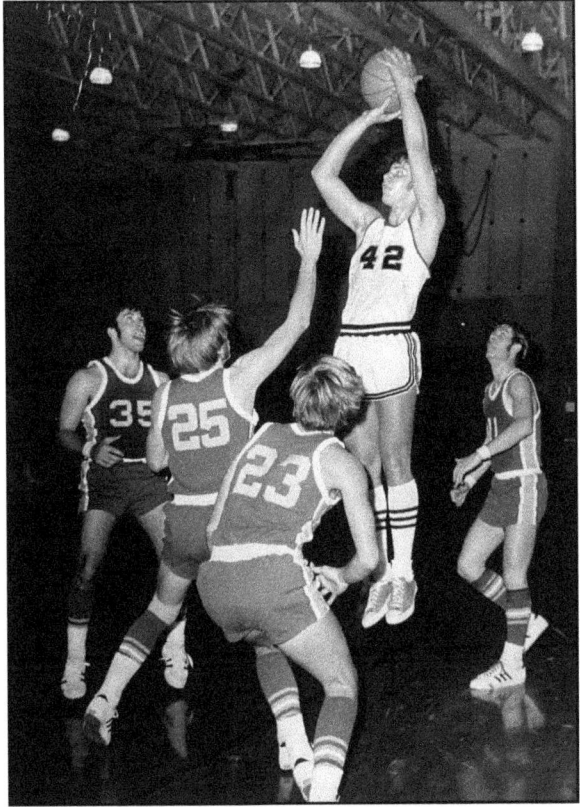

Mark's basketball shot.

Sue was always there.

"I remember looking up into the stands and watching her from the basketball floor," Mark said. "One night I got cramps in both legs and lay on the floor in pain. Both Sue and my mom reacted strongly in the stands."

"I remember standing up," Sue said, "just praying for him to get up."

"Another time in a track meet, I hit a hurdle and went down hard on the cinder track we had. Sue literally picked the cinders out of my legs and bandaged up the cuts. After the sporting events, Sue and I would either go to her place where her mom had Schwan pizzas or to my house where my mom would always have way too much food...many times hot ham with chips and dip."

"I always wondered how so much food would just appear," Sue said.

Their friends would often join them at the Neumanns, though not usually if the celebration was at Sue's house. "Then it would be just Mark and me," she said.

* * * * *

Summertime activities for the Neumanns and Links included Milwaukee shopping trips and the annual Fourth of July East Troy Carnival. "Sue and I had many good times there," Mark said.

"The summer before I had my driver's license, Sue came with my family to Brookfield Square for a shopping trip. Before heading home we stopped at what I believe was one of the first McDonald's in Milwaukee."

Mark has always held Joseph Link in high regard. "Sue's dad was so smart and patient."

"He had to be, to milk fifty to sixty Holstein cows," Sue added. Milk production is quite a science. Not only does the dairy farmer have to sell the milk, but must also keep the product at a particular temperature until it is picked up by a milk hauler. Cows had to be bred in order to keep up milk production, and the calves were either raised or sold. The cows needed to be fed, and raising crops was important. They rotated corn, hay and wheat.

As time went on and Joseph was ready to give up farming, David and Alan, Sue's younger brothers, took over for a while. Then the bottom went out of the dairy market and running a mid-sized family farm could no longer support the families. There was an auction to sell the cows and machinery.

"Dad felt bad," Sue said. Her brother Dave has horses on some of the property and boards them. Alan lives on part of the farm as well and operates a tree farm.

A non-secret in the neighborhood was that part of the farm, known as Link's Field, was a party place where kids gathered for fun. "The police would wake my dad in the middle of the night and ask, 'Do you know there's a big party going on in your field?' and he'd laugh and say, sure he knew. Better the kids were there than out on the streets getting into trouble."

Mark and Sue have fond memories of the place, too. "One winter when my brother was at the Air Force Academy," Mark said. "I had decided to go out and to ski with him during our spring break. The night before leaving, Sue and I went out to the field. This particular night the ground was soft and we got stuck. After trying everything we could think of we did the unthinkable...we walked to the neighbor's house and we called Sue's dad, getting him out of bed, I might add. He calmly got on a tractor and came down and pulled us out. Then, rather than yell at us, he got out the water hose and cleaned off the car so my parents would not find out. Have patience, stay calm, and take care of others willingly. Another lesson learned."

* * * * *

THE GREEN 1964 IMPALA

When Mark was fifteen, before he could actually drive, he was "encouraged" to put money in to help big brother Dave buy a car...big brother, of course, was actually doing the driving.

"I don't think you ever drove that car, did you?" Sue asked.

"No," Mark said. "Dave's logic was that I got rides to school out of the deal. I didn't have to take the bus, so I got to help pay for the car."

Having Dave drive to various after-school activities made life a little easier for Kurt and Stella. "Dad got a discount through his job at General Motors," Mark said. Mark used this discount to buy new cars with dollars earned later while working. He had several Vega models and eventually bought a yellow Camaro after he and Sue were married and living in Whitewater. "That was a beautiful car," Mark said.

Once Mark got his driver's license, he would often head out to see Sue after work. "It was late, but where there was a will, there was a way...and it worked out okay. Her parents were great, understanding the work thing and my showing up late at their place."

The first motorcycle story is short and sweet. The summer between their junior and senior years of high school, Mark bought a Honda 90 to save money commuting to work. "It was fun to drive. I'd take Highway 20 to work at Linden Terrace, tie and all, through East Troy. The speed limit was about thirty miles an hour. A pickup pulled out from a stop sign and hit me square."

Mark recalled the event as if it had happened to someone else. "The motorcycle ended up flattened underneath the truck and I ended up twenty feet away, standing upright, looking at it. Talk about a miracle!"

"You, what, only hurt your finger? And had bumps and bruises?" Sue said.

"Right. Only my finger. I called Sue to tell her, and she said—"

"No more cycles, Honey. And we didn't...until we moved to Lake Country in 2000 and bought a Harley."

LINDEN TERRACE YEARS

Mark had a good friend, Lee Hammerling, whose family owned Linden Terrace, a supper club on Booth Lake. While Mark was still in junior high, Lee asked if he would be interested in bussing tables a couple nights a week after working on the farm. "I would head to Linden Terrace after the farm and bus for a few hours," Mark said of the start of long, respectful experience with the restaurant and its owners. Starting the following summer, he worked full time on the Priefer farm plus extra hours for the Hammerlings, and this continued even after marriage.

Linden Terrace, where our wedding was held while Mark Still worked there.

"Joan Hammerling, my boss, was great about working our hours around any sporting activities, whether it was a Friday night game or summer practices for football," Mark said.

Joan Hammerling had taken over an old former hotel in 1962 and turned it into a popular restaurant and meeting place for the next several decades, serving Friday night Wisconsin fish fry dinners.

"A typical day for me included starting early on outside work and/or stocking the bar," Mark said. "We built numerous Lannon stone walls with literally tons and tons of stone. These walls created beautiful terraces overlooking Booth Lake, hence Linden Terrace."

Some of the outdoor work was with homes on the Linden Terrace premises. "I have a vivid memory of a scaffolding giving way and falling about eight feet to the ground," Mark shared. "Paint went everywhere!

"By about 10:30 in the morning, we would clean up and head inside to work the noon lunch crowd in the restaurant, take a couple hours off to enjoy the lake, and then go back for the dinner crowd. The restaurant work included cleaning, stocking bar, bussing tables in the beginning, and then later waiting on tables and tending bar. I would work most Friday and Saturday nights and many times a Sunday brunch after church. Typically, I would work five days per week in the restaurant. This was how we spent our high school summers.

"They treated me great and I learned so much from them in terms of how to treat others. They made sure I had the hours of work I wanted. We all understood how restaurants work. But they also taught me again about how hard work leads to success. I watched them put in endless hours to make the place work and be one of the most respected businesses in East Troy. Joan gave us incentives. She had the most delicious food and said we could eat all we wanted after the dining room was ready for the next day. Three of us could set a dinner room so fast!"

One of the Linden Terrace regulars made an impact on Mark during his high school years. "I served him all the time, and one day, he took me aside and told me to be a salesman. 'Work on commission. That way, the harder you work, the more you will be paid.'

"A second principle he instilled in me was that as long as I worked for someone else, that person or business had to make money off of me working for them...obviously if they lost money employing me, the business would cease to exist.

"These two principles stuck with me and influenced me. They became a voice in my head as I made life decisions to enter real estate sales and eventually start our own businesses."

More principles about developing and maintaining work relationships deeply influenced Mark from his experience with the Hammerlings. "Whether it was interacting with the public, usually in a positive way but at times with difficult, unreasonable people, or simply working side by side with the employees, the Hammerlings always treated everyone fairly. Creating this 'family' work setting, along with working just as hard as they expected us to work, would become a cornerstone in creating and growing our future businesses."

Joan's brother and sister-in law, Jim and Faye Rice, shared responsibilities. "All four of them worked very hard all the time during the restaurant years," Mark said. Joan's husband, Emil, passed away at age forty-two. Mark recalls being in college. "It was a very traumatic time. He was my best friend Lee's father."

Jim Rice passed away at age forty-four while Mark and Sue were living in River Falls. "He was my mentor," Mark said.

* * * * *

During the winter months, Mark and Sue worked at Alpine Valley Ski Resort, south of East Troy. "Sue worked in the ski shop while I worked in the restaurant," Mark said. "The winter months were the slow months at Linden Terrace and I could almost always work a Saturday and Sunday shift.

"One night on her way home, Sue totaled her dad's car. I remember getting the call and being really scared. She was crying so I went over to her place...thank God she was okay. Her dad, the saint, simply said, 'Thank God you weren't hurt.' It was, again, an important lesson on how to react; however, the part that did get her in trouble with her dad was the fact that she stood out on the road when two men stopped to help and gave her a ride home."

Sue also worked at the local burger shop as a waitress. One night after closing, a co-worker was crying so Sue took her home without sweeping the floor as she was supposed to do. "The next day, my boss called and swore at me on the phone. Dad never let me go back. I still remember him saying, 'Any man who swears at my daughter is never going to have her work for him again.'"

Joseph Link developed heart disease later in life and was not expected to live very long when diagnosed in the mid-nineties. "I remember the doctor called us into the office and showed us a picture of his heart," Mark said. "They told us he was not going to make it very long." He lived another nine years before passing on in August of 2007.

SENIOR YEAR – JUNE 1971-JUNE 1972

Mark's parents thought he should read and comprehend as well as his older brother, Dave, who seemed to be able to churn out excellent grades with little effort, "so smart he never cracked a book and earned A's all the time," according to Mark. "They thought Dave could read a lot faster, so they believed if I could read faster that would solve my academic problems (getting some B's mixed in with the A's). So on top of all his other activities, Mark was sent to the Evelyn Wood Reading Dynamics Institute at 208 East Wisconsin Avenue in Milwaukee in the summer of 1971. All summer, once a week, Mark attended a workshop with other people who attempted to take advantage of speedreading techniques.

The course had been created by former high school teacher Evelyn Wood (1909-1995) in 1959 and soon became a national fad, promoted in many public schools and used by at three presidents who sent cabinet members to take the course. Courses are still available.

Sue said. "I remember you being mad you had to go."

"I know I wasn't happy about it," Mark said. "But in hindsight, I know my parents did everything they could to make sure we were successful."

Academically, Mark's high school reports show an average in the lower 90-out-of-100 range, which was high B/low A in most subjects, with his highest scores usually in math.

FIRST ELECTED OFFICE

Mark was selected to attend the Badger Boys State Conference from June 12 to 19, 1971, sponsored by the American Legion. Mark's acceptance letter was signed by Edward Ormsby, Commander, American Legion.

Badger Boys State is an intensive one-week summer camp for young men (young women can attend Badger Girls State) between their junior and senior years of high school. The camp experience gives young people the opportunity to learn more about government and how to be better leaders. The Wisconsin American Legion has sponsored the program at Ripon College since 1941.

Upon arrival, the boys, or citizens, were grouped into cities and counties which form a "51st state." They carry out all the main functions of city, county, and state government using laws of the State of Wisconsin as a guide.

Mark was elected mayor of the city of Harvey. "What I really remember is I didn't like it because Sue wasn't there. It

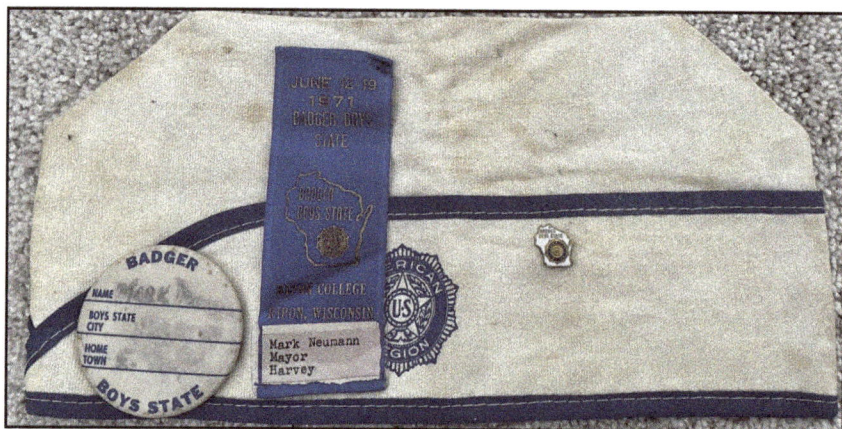

Badger Boys State memorabilia, 1971.

was after we had started going steady again. There was a statewide election for lieutenant governor that I tried for and didn't win. Then I ran for mayor and was elected. There were lots of meetings, participating in groups where we heard talks by different people, including the then-governor, Patrick J. Lucey. I remember it as a place where things were run in an orderly fashion, not out of place."

Because of his attendance, he received an undated form letter from West Point Military Academy, inviting him to apply as a cadet.

Mark and Sue sent dozens of letters back and forth during this time. He sent three letters from the week he was at Ripon. Immediately following was a Lutheran Pioneers trip to the Boundary Waters. More letters went to Sue from Ely, Minnesota, including a note with his address where she could send letters to him while he was up at camp. The letter-writing continued during their year apart after high school graduation.

* * * * *

Mark continued to be active in sports, particularly football and basketball.

He was voted Most Valuable Player in basketball and the best free-thrower of the team, over which he and Lee Hammerling were co-team captains. He was named to the Second All Conference Basketball team in the Western Division of Southern Lakes. Mark saved posters and newspaper articles from his games. On Mom's Night, February 8, 1972, senior year, he made five buckets, four free throws, led in rebounds, and was fouled three times. Maybe his mom's showing up in a hot pink mini-

Newsclip of All Conference Basketball Team.

dress and white go-go boots that had his teammates whispering helped distract the opponents.

With a new coach, the East Troy Trojans weren't exactly championship material those years, with a record of 6 and 12.

THE DRAFT

"Dear Registrant, you have been placed in Class 1H,
new classification for those not subject to induction…"
Signed M. Shaw, Executive Secretary

When he turned eighteen, Mark received his Selective Service System letter, Walworth County Board 73. Selective Service was one of the scarier non-academic terms tossed about those days.

"The draft was a very big deal," he said. "It was earth-shattering for those who were drafted. I remember sitting in class when one of my classmate's number was called. It was very bad if one received a low number, as he was likely headed to the very unpopular Vietnam War."

Mark drew a high number, so he was pretty sure he wasn't going to be called up as the conflict was winding down. His birth year lottery would have been called in March 1973 had the draft continued, "but I didn't know that then," he said.

SELECTIVE SERVICE SYSTEM

WALWORTH CO. LOCAL BD. 73
SELECTIVE SERVICE SYSTEM
1ST NATL BANK, 19 N WIS ST
ELKHORN, WI 53121

(LOCAL BOARD STAMP)

Dear Registrant,

The enclosed notification advises you that you have been placed in Class 1-H. This is a new administrative classification for those registrants who are not currently subject to processing for induction. If your lottery number is high enough, you will be left in Class 1-H indefinitely, with the realization that each year your likelihood of being selected for induction is decreasing.

If at any future time, your lottery number and priority group fall in the range of those being selected for induction, you will be reclassified out of 1-H. At that time, you will have the opportunity to present any claim for deferment and you will be classified into an appropriate class. You will also have the procedural rights of personal appearance and appeal during the 15-day period following the issuance of the notice that you have been reclassified.

As a 1-H registrant, you are required to inform the local board of any change in your address. However, it will not be necessary for you to inform the local board of any change in your occupational, marital, family, or dependency status or of your physical condition until such time as your local board requests further information.

By direction of the local board

Exec. Secy

Mark's Selective Service letter.

THE DANCES

Mark and Sue's boxes of memorabilia include saved garters—white with pink, green, and light blue. They went with Sue's prom dresses, which she kept, preserved in plastic wrap, fresh as when they were worn last. There were no prom pictures from freshman year as they didn't attend that dance.

"Sophomore prom was the blue dress," Sue said. The big break-up occurred after that prom.

By junior year prom, they were back together...that was the lovely, lacy white dress. Mark wore a white tux. And would you believe senior year? Senior prom. "Mark's favorite color was green," Sue said. "I can't stand the color green. Guess what I had my mother make for Mark? A green dress."

Sue's Prom dresses and garters, worn sophomore, junior, and senior year with Mark.

Mark and Sue, Junior
Prom, 1971.

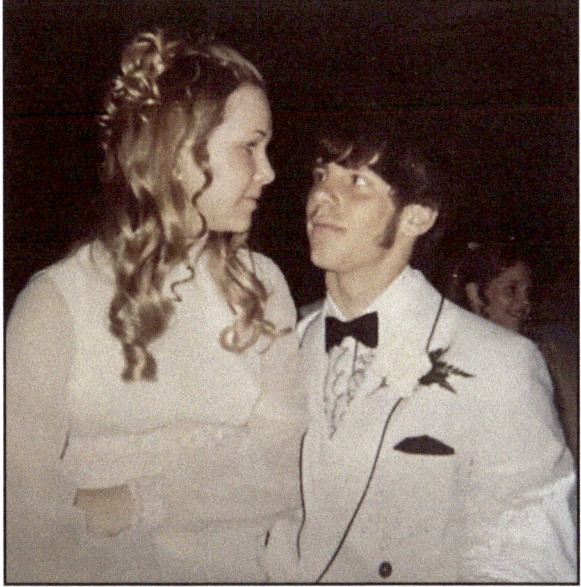

Mark grins but stays quiet while Sue shares the memory. "He was not going to wear a tux that year. He said he didn't think he needed a tux—"

"Too much money," Mark cut in.

"But he surprised me and rented a green tux that matched my dress. Mom told him the color."

"Just for you, Honey," he said.

"Though we clashed." Sue laughed. "I remember when he showed up at the door, thinking, *oh, no*. But there we were."

Years later, Mark said that because Sue liked to take cruises on the Cunard line because of the dress-up rule, he signed them up for dance lessons before they went on the first cruise so he could dance with her.

The proms involved extra activities besides the dance. "One year we had a picnic in poison ivy," Mark said. "We got poison

Sue in Green Prom dress, Senior Prom, 1972.

ivy all over us. We'd set our blanket right in poison ivy. We were too dumb to know better."

There had once been pictures of their rivals at Homecoming during the break-up year, but those were dealt with as Mark and Sue revisited their memories.

By their senior year, they were back together for their final High School Homecoming dance.

Both Mark and Sue were active in many extra-curricular activities during their high school years. The 1972 supplement to the yearbook lists Mark in forensics—state winner. "Forensics was on Saturdays," Mark said. He won the Mike Norton Scholarship, named for a high school classmate. "Mike died of a heart ailment our senior year while running track," Mark said. "And I

Mark and Sue, Home coming senior year.

won the scholarship." He had been a good friend, and the loss was hard.

Mark and Sue were also involved with the senior class play, *The White Sheep of the Family*, by L. duGarde Peach and Jan Hay. Performances were held December 4 and 5, 1971. Sue worked on the stage crew, and in makeup, and publicity, while Mark played the Vicar, a comedic role.

Their saved papers and report cards reflect their forward-thinking and wise school choices in both academics and future-preparedness. Mark kept several English papers with scores average to high on titles such as *Comparing The Grapes of Wrath and Lord of the Flies*, along with reports on other classics. Sue was inducted into the National Honor Society in 1971.

Mark and Sue at the senior homecoming dance, 1971.

FUTURE HOMEMAKERS OF AMERICA

Sue's main non-academic activity was with Future Homemakers of America, which she participated in every year of high school. "That was my thing," she said. "I enjoyed that—cooking and sewing. I was in a class with my peers and friends. I distinctly remember a class on how to bathe a baby. I remember thinking, 'I'm going to do this someday.'"

She was also in Bowling Club, National Honor Society, and Pep Club, according to the yearbook photos. And she was on the yearbook staff. By senior year, she added Ski Club to her schedule, probably due to her boyfriend's coaxing, but she hardly remembered participating. Attendance-wise, she was usually out sick about a week or more each academic year.

Mark was vice president of the Ski Club, in the Photography Club and National Honor Society. Lee Hammerling was president of the Ski Club. Lee also served as class president. Mark was in French Club all four years, and on Student Council, was involved in the Photo Club, which mainly took pictures for the yearbook. He was on the Debate team and Letterman's Club, Pep Club, and various musical groups. He enjoyed theater, and besides the senior class play, was also in *Annie Get Your Gun* in his junior year.

HIGH SCHOOL YEARBOOKS

Mark and Sue's high school yearbooks are typical, full of fond memories, and those signatures carrying so much friendship, love, and angst. Mark didn't sign Sue's book until junior year, a lengthy epistle stating, "The happiest moment of my life was when you said you'd go steady with me."

Sue signed inside Mark's front page, a long note about hoping to work somehow, having a good time this summer and looking forward to next year. Sue starts her senior yearbook with a sweet note that says, "You have made life worth living for me, Mark, and I know that we cannot live without each other, so next

Mark and Sue kept all their high school yearbooks.

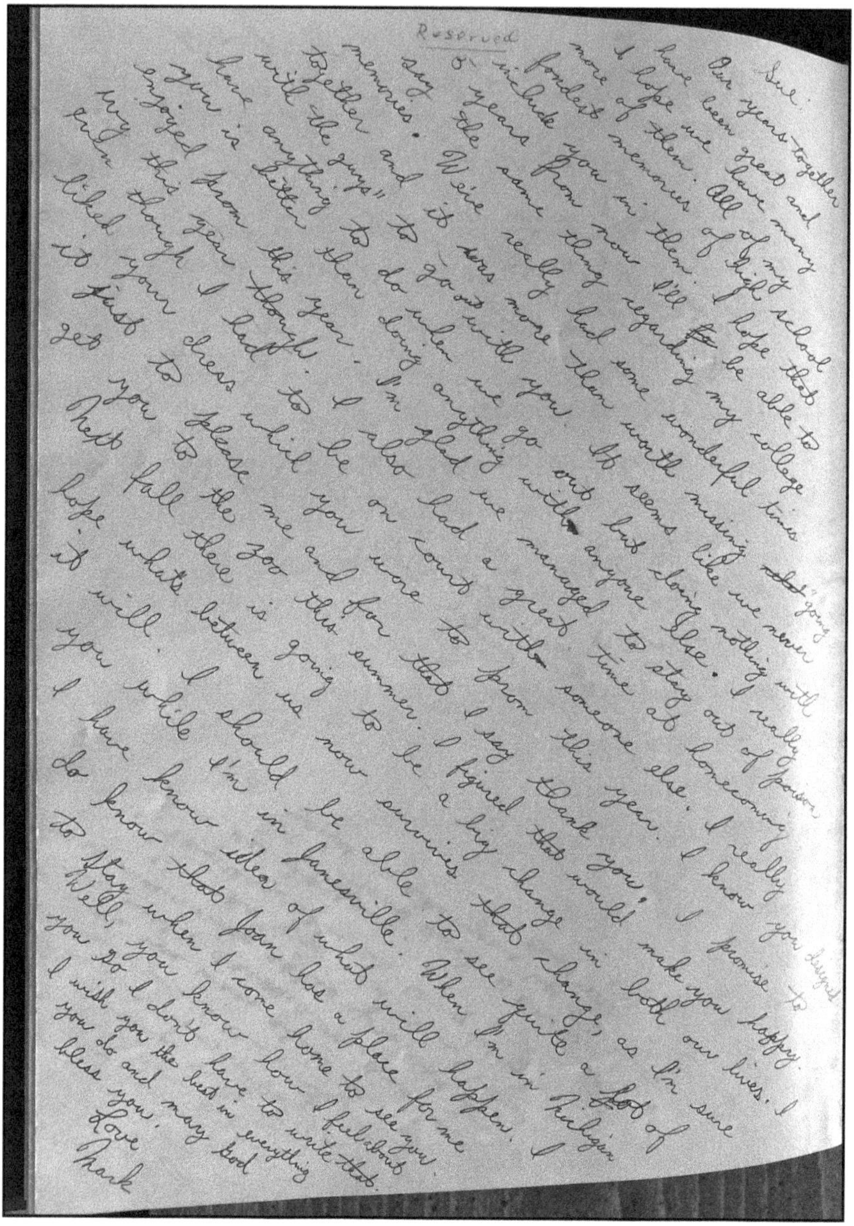

Reserved

Sue:
Our years together
have been great and
I hope we have many
more of them. All of my
fondest memories of high school
include you in them. I hope that
years from now I'll be able to
say the same thing regarding my college
memories. We've really had some wonderful times
together and it's been more than worth missing "going
with the guys" to go out with you. It seems like we never
have anything to do when we go out but doing nothing with
you is better than doing anything with anyone else. I really
enjoyed prom this year. I'm glad we managed to stay out of prison
my this though. I also had a great time at homecoming
even though I had to be on court with someone else. I really
liked your dress which you wore to prom this year. I know you designed
it just to please me and for that I say thank you. I promise to
get you to the zoo this summer. I figured that would make you happy.
Next fall there is going to be a big change in both our lives. I
hope whats between us now survives that change, as I'm sure
it will. I should be able to see quite a lot of
you while I'm in Janesville. When I'm in Michigan
I have know idea of what will happen. I
do know Joan has a place for me
to stay when I come home to see you.
Well, you know how I feel about
you so I don't have to write.
I wish you the best in everything
you do and may God
bless you.
Love
Mark

Mark's senior yearbook signing to Sue.

Reserved (for whom?)

Mark,
I don't know why
you wanted a whole page
for me, because there can't
really that much to say. I mean
I tell you everything the moment it
exists, so there isn't much more to say. Mark,
this year has been the best year that I've ever
had. You couldn't have made it more enjoyable for me.
Whenever I had a problem that couldn't be talked over with
just anyone, I knew I could count on you to always be there
when I needed anything. Whenever I felt that life just wasn't
worth it, I would just think of you, and I'd immediately change
my mind. Things have really been hard to cope with at times, like
when I would always feel sick because of those certain times a
month. But worse than that were the times when I was really sick,
like for graduation! And then if I wasn't sick during those important
occasions, I would find a way to be sick for at least 2 weeks after.
(like both proms). But then you were always there to keep me going, even
though I felt like dieing any second. Mark, I really thank you for
all of the wonderful things you've done for me. Like when you decided to
rent a tux for prom, and surprised me with it. I couldn't have been
happier. And remember that time at a certain someone's birthday, when
you brought 100 pieces of kielbasa? I even had the nerve to think that
you had only gotten me that. But then you surprised me again with that
beautiful sweater! Another thing that I'll never forget is when you tell
me all about hunting, and stupid, gullible me, always believed every
word, until finally you backed down and laughed at me for being so
stupid. I am usually so amazed at my stupidity that even I
laugh at myself. Well Mark, I'm at the end of the page, so
I'll just say that I'll try my hardest to not yell at you,
(unless you deserve it) and I'll try to not walk hard
JUST KIDDING
on my heels, which I know you hate. You
have made life worth living for me, Mark,
and I know that we cannot live
without each other ever, so
next year you will have to see
each other often, right?
All my love
always,
Sue

Sue's senior yearbook signing to Mark.

year we have to see each other often, right? All my love, always, Sue."

Mark: "Well, you know how I feel about you so I don't have to write that. I wish you the best in everything you do and may God bless you. Love, Mark."

* * * * *

Mark, like most other college-bound seniors, had applied to several institutions, including both naval and air force academies, and the University of Wisconsin-Whitewater. His acceptance letter to UW-Whitewater from the College of Letters and Sciences was dated March 24, 1972.

"It came down to money," Mark said of his final choice, a work study program at General Motors Institute (later Kettering University) in Flint, Michigan.

He was placed on the reserve lists of the military academies and later received appointments to both the Naval Academy and the Air Force Academy, but decided to stay with the GMI decision.

LUTHERAN PIONEERS

During his school years, Mark and his brothers were in Lutheran Pioneers, a chartered organization similar to Girl and Boy Scouts. Mark achieved the Voyager, Red Beret title, a high accomplishment in the Outdoorsmen category of concentration. Lutheran Pioneers had separate groups for girls and boys. "The purpose of the group was to instill a sense of teamwork," Mark said.

In order to qualify for the big trips, canoe trips to the Boundary Waters in Minnesota, for example, the Pioneers mastered different skills, such as learning how to tie a number of knots, how to set up a tent, cook over a campfire—

"No wonder you don't like to grill out," Sue quipped.

Mark was honored to meet Commander Bruce Thompson and his son Steve from Burlington, Wisconsin. Bruce started the concept of Lutheran Pioneers, which has spread across the country.

Pioneers met once a week at church during the school year, while the trips were summertime activities. Mark recalled about fifteen boys in his group, kids from all over who attended different Lutheran churches.

"It was a lot of work, including two canoe trips to the Boundary Waters in Canada," Mark said.

The first trip was in 1969. "My canoe partner was Eric Hogenson. You're the newcomer on the first trip, and after, you become a Red Beret. On the second summer trip, there are more options, so you can pick and choose the activities. I spent more time fishing on the second trip."

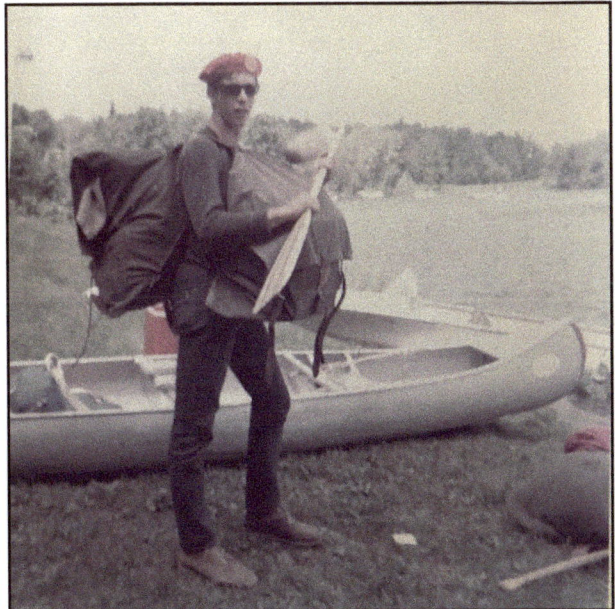

Voyageur trip to the Boundary Waters.

The second trip was in 1970, the summer between sophomore and junior year of high school. Mark attended the week-long Voyageur Camp, June 16-19.

During the canoe trip in Canada, the boys caught, cooked, and ate a lot of fish, sometimes for every meal. A great many photographs were sent to all the boys afterward. Mark sent a postcard home from Ely, Minnesota, "Dear Dad (& Mom), we made it up here all right."

Mark recalled one of the trips during which he learned another valuable lesson about teamwork and caring for each other. "We were on a trip out of camp in the middle of a large bay and a strong wind suddenly came up, as often happens. I will never forget my paddle breaking in two. We were seriously in trouble until one of the other canoes with an extra paddle managed to catch us and hand me off a second paddle so we could make it off the bay."

The broken paddle.

* * * * *

Through Mark's senior year in high school was an undercurrent of change at General Motors, Kurt and Stella's employers. Production was shifting, and eventually the elder Neumanns were offered transfers. Unfortunately the transfers were not to the same plant, or even the same state. Stella was offered a position in Kokomo, Indiana, and Kurt a job in Santa Barbara, California. They could either move or take a layoff.

They took a "Mutual Separation Agreement," sold the Lake Beulah house, and moved to Colorado, without a job or even a permanent location in mind. Their oldest son David had received a full-ride scholarship and appointment to the Air Force Academy in Colorado Springs. Kurt and Stella packed up the youngest children, Connie, Ken, and Kathy, and moved. The move meant that after Mark graduated from high school, he was on his own.

"The Hammerlings were so good to us, and Sue was here," Mark said.

Mark receiving his diploma from Mr. Cox with Sue watching.

THE YEAR OF DECISION—

POST HIGH SCHOOL, 1972-1973

Mark and Sue graduated from East Troy High School in a ceremony held June 9, 1972. Both were honor students.

Sue was all set, knowing what she would do. She went to Racine for the medical assistant program at Gateway Technical Institute, one of twenty-four students in her class. Sue had saved enough money to pay the first semester of school on her own, and "Dad 'loaned' me the rest." Beverly and Joe moved her in at the YMCA downtown, since there wasn't a Young Women's Christian Association in Racine. They thought it would be safe, and the top floor was reserved for women.

"'Interesting' people lived there," Sue said. She had a miniscule room, 611, and shared the communal bathroom with others in the hall. Fortunately, a girl who lived next door became a very good friend. "We walked to school together, and took meals together. There was a restaurant on the main floor where we had vouchers to eat." After the first semester, she told her parents she didn't want to stay at the Y anymore and went to live in a rented house on College Avenue with five girls for the second semester.

That year of near-separation was filled with loneliness for both Mark and Sue on many levels. They wrote to each other often, sometimes daily, sending letters back and forth with news about their day and activities, fears, love, and hopes. Mark sent Sue flowers and pining missives. Sue sent airmail letters to him all the way over in Flint, Michigan, and brownies "at the risk of punishment by death" from her dad and brothers.

Sue's program included courses in chemistry, biology, lab technique, medical assistant functions, medical terminology,

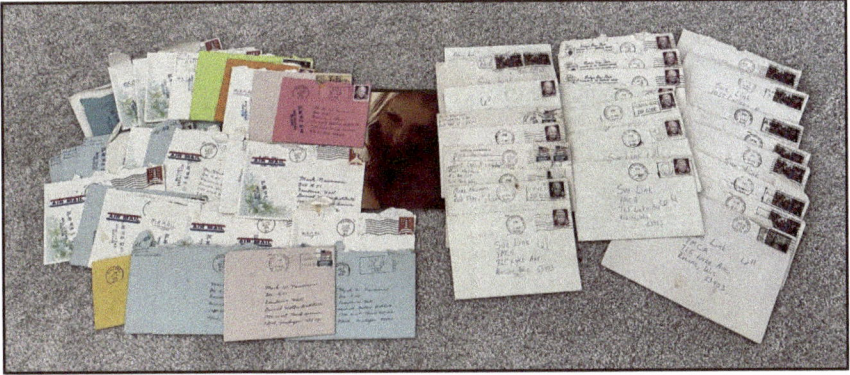

Letters written to each other while in college.

Sue's grades at Gateway.

Sue's graduation from Gateway with two closest friends, Jane and Carol.

clinic office function, and social behavior. She maintained a 4.0 throughout the course.

"I would come home and look at Sue's schedule," Mark said. "I thought her chemistry courses were way harder than what I was taking." He was using a slide rule at his college—no calculators back then. Still, Mark helped Sue where he could.

"We had to figure out how much dosage of medication to give," she said. "It was very important stuff. One thing I recall was the course where I was training as a doctor's assistant to hand him material, and how to draw blood and give shots, I knew that was going to be hard, so I thought, 'I'm just going to have to get through it and do it.' That's why I didn't sign up to be a nurse. When given a challenge, you just have to rise to meet it.

"Everyone wanted to practice drawing blood on me because my veins are very deep and you have to feel for them. We practiced on each other, and some of us brought in our boyfriends. Mark never did that. I became very good friends with these women who were such a close-knit group being in classes together all day, every day. I am still Christmas-card friends with some of them."

Sue graduated as valedictorian in her class with her degree in the Medical Assistant Program in May of 1973, with recognition for excellence in academic achievement. In the class photo, she wore a white uniform dress.

Stella and Kurt, Mark's parents, sent her a lovely card and note on her graduation, *"Congratulations to our future Daughter-in-law! Signed, Mark's Dad and Mother."*

The graduation ceremony wasn't quite the end. Sue still had to do a six-week internship after graduation. She completed her program at clinic in Elkhorn. Sue took her first job after school as

Sue's graduating class at Gateway, 1973.

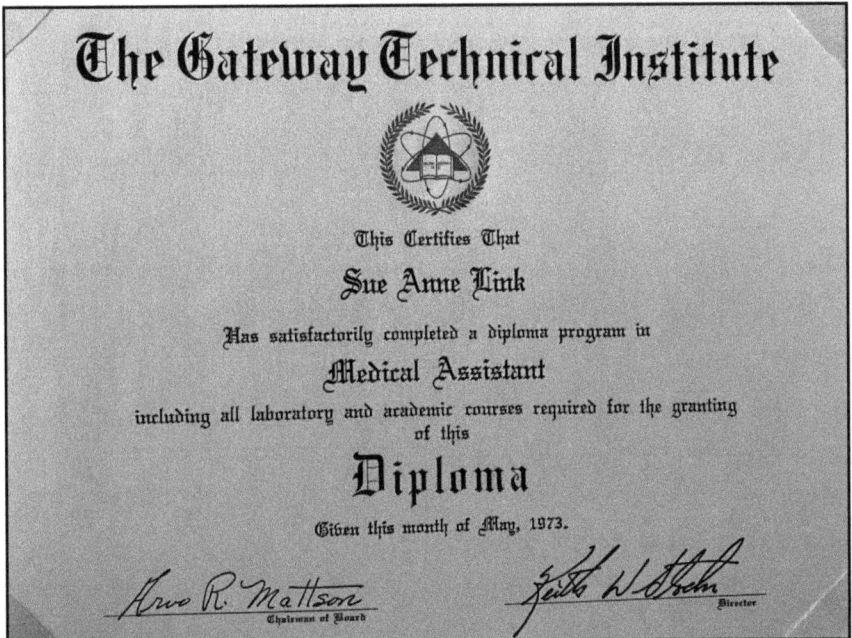

The Gateway Technical Institute

This Certifies That

Sue Anne Link

Has satisfactorily completed a diploma program in

Medical Assistant

including all laboratory and academic courses required for the granting
of this

Diploma

Given this month of May, 1973.

Arvo R. Mattson
Chairman of Board

Keith W. Stohr
Director

Sue's diploma: Medical Assistant degree.

a ward clerk at Fairhaven Senior Center in Whitewater, where she continued to work after marriage. Sue worked in the field at various places for eight years, both full-time and part-time.

* * * * *

Mark applied to and was accepted as an engineering student at General Motors Institute in Flint, Michigan, in a work-study program. Mark went to school six weeks, and worked in the Janesville General Motors plant for six weeks to pay for the six weeks of school. He lasted a semester.

"I wasn't cut out to be an engineer," Mark said. "Math is very different from engineering. And I missed Sue."

Much of the disillusionment over the engineering was the six weeks on the job. "It was not a very pleasant experience," Mark said. "Here I was, this punk kid in a tie—they made me wear a suit and a tie."

Cars would come down the assembly line with a six- or eight-page report attached to them outlining all the defects. "I would have to count all the defects and put them on a master schedule while workers up the line had to stop and work on the defect." Apparently, the workers who'd been there years had a system all set up that allowed them to work ahead on up to fifteen cars so they could take a break. "There I was, standing there, an eighteen-year-old kid in a tie, next to union workers telling them what to do. I was messing up their operation—in their minds. I was much younger, much less experienced, disrupting those people who had been there years."

At the plant, Mark didn't fare any better with a switch from the assembly line defect situation to a job in the paint room. In the paint room, he was to use an expensive machine to accurately measure the moisture content of paint before it was applied to the cars. "I found out this person who had been operating the machine didn't actually know how to use it. I was put into a position to explain to him that he was missing the final step...I couldn't stand it. I didn't like the relationships that were not built because of what I was forced to do."

Despite some of the good times at the Institute, like learning to play the card game Pinochle and meeting some good people, Mark's memories were of the loneliness. "I remember on Sundays I'd go to church with my friends and on the way home, I'd pick up some fast food and sit in my room and study."

"Your parents had just moved and I was across the lake in Racine," Sue said. "I'd be over there, thinking, he's across the lake. We missed each other so much."

Using a slide rule was a source of frustration too. "I was a true math person and the slide rule was just too imprecise—at least, it was when I used it. I didn't like that at all. The people who were coming there from both the East and West coasts were substantially ahead of me in engineering abilities. It was the era of hair down to your shoulders. Engineering wasn't what I wanted to do, it wasn't who I was."

Mark had always wanted to teach school, and decided to turn in a different direction for his secondary education. And he missed Sue...

"Mark just wanted to be home," Sue said.

"She used to call me and say how long it would be until we could see each other again. But she counts differently than I do. She doesn't count the week we're in, or the week we'd see each other, so she'd say something like, 'It's four weeks until you come home,' when it was really six."

Mark would then take the long ride around Lake Michigan to come home for the weekend. Only "home" now meant the

Hammerling's basement, since his parents had moved to Colorado. "After my parents were gone, Joan took care of me, and fixed me meals," Mark said.

"It wasn't anything like today, with cell phones and Internet," Sue said. "Mark didn't have a phone in his rooms, and he'd have to wait for a call or for the phone in the hallway to be free to use it. And long distance was terribly expensive—we had no money."

"This is how awful those long car trips were," Mark said. "I don't smoke, but on those six-hour trips, I would smoke cigarettes to stay awake."

"He'd bring me his laundry," Sue said. "I'd send him back with brownies or cookies. That was where my home ec experience came in handy."

The Hammerling family regularly went on vacation at the end of November. "The only week they would close the restaurant was on Mondays and Thanksgiving week," Mark said. He knew they would be gone when he came back for the Thanksgiving break in 1972. He parked in the driveway and was fast asleep in the basement when a noise woke him...to the sight of a policeman's pistol pointed at his nose.

"What are you doing here?" the officer yelled.

An explanation led to an eventual apology, and all was fine after a while.

By this time Mark had enough of being on his own and was ready to not only come home, but make one with Sue. He asked for her hand in marriage that Christmas in 1972.

ENGAGING TIMES

"My mom was shocked," Sue said, when told the news back at home. Sue was only eighteen and halfway through her medical assistant training.

"My parents were happy," Mark said. "They asked why we wanted to wait until August to get married."

"That's because they'd moved," Sue said. "My parents wanted me to wait until I was twenty to get married. But they could see that I loved Mark."

"We talked her mom into it," Mark said.

"But then she was worried because she only had eight months to plan," Sue said. Soon after, Sue's brother Joe got engaged and set an October wedding date. "Later Mom would say it was good we married young so we'd have all these years together."

That February, for Mark's birthday, Sue asked him what kind of a cake she could make for him.

"I told her I liked banana cake," Mark said. "It's so moist and gooey."

Banana cake became a tradition. Even if they're away on Mark's actual birthday, the family celebrates with banana cake when Mark and Sue are home. "Now the grandkids like to pile the whole top with candles and make it hard to blow them out."

BACK TO SCHOOL IN JANUARY OF 1973

Mark left the Institute to transfer to the University of Wisconsin–Whitewater, where he'd been accepted before his high school graduation.

"He is the potter," Mark said, referring to his favorite Bible verse, speaking of the Lord. "He decided to reshape the pottery He was making."

Mark returned to his first desire, becoming a high school math teacher, and coaching sports.

PART TWO
FAITH, FAMILY, BUSINESS
1973-1989

"Sue and I started with nothing except each other and our faith."
—Mark Neumann

Mark and Sue's wedding, August 18, 1973

THEN COMES MARRIAGE AND FAMILY 1973-1979

THE WEDDING

Mark and Sue's wedding was set for August 18, 1973, a 2 p.m. ceremony at St. Paul's Lutheran Church in East Troy. The wedding had to be in the summer between school semesters if they were going to get married before Mark's graduation.

Typical of the bridegroom part of the wedding plans, Mark had little to do. He wanted to choose the flowers Sue carried in her bouquet. Sue thought she should decide on the flowers, and they compromised by picking the bouquet together.

Since the dinner was held at Mark's place of work, he chose the food—ham and beef and mashed potatoes. The Friday night rehearsal dinner was at the Linden Terrace too.

"Joan was running a little behind," Mark recalled. "She sent great big platters of fresh shrimp to the tables as a surprise, and made everyone happy. Then they didn't mind running late.

"Joan did the wedding dinner," Mark said. "She did a great job. We filled the place and had a great family-style meal."

"I remember waking up on Saturday morning," Sue said, "and it was raining. I thought, *Oh no, it's going to be a rainy day for the wedding*. I had long hair back then, and went to the beauty shop in the morning. It was so hot and humid out. I remember having my hair curled and sitting under the dryer forever. It was taking so long for my hair to dry. Then, in the humidity, my hair started straightening out by the time I got home."

"Now wait a minute!" Mark cut in. "Sue's one of those people whose too hard on herself. Your hair was just perfect."

"You didn't care, you just wanted to get married," Sue said, and they both laughed. "I polished my nails—it was back in the day when you did that yourself." Sue's friend Deborah Zinn was maid of honor.

The groom and his attendants dressed at Lee Hammerling's house. Lee served as best man. Mark's older brother Dave thought it would be funny to fiddle with Mark's car. "He took something out of the engine so it wouldn't start," Mark said. "He knew what he was doing. But then he fixed it. One last shot at splitting us up!"

Sue holding bouquet.

Mark and Sue at the church window.

Mark and Sue toast at Linden Terrace dinner.

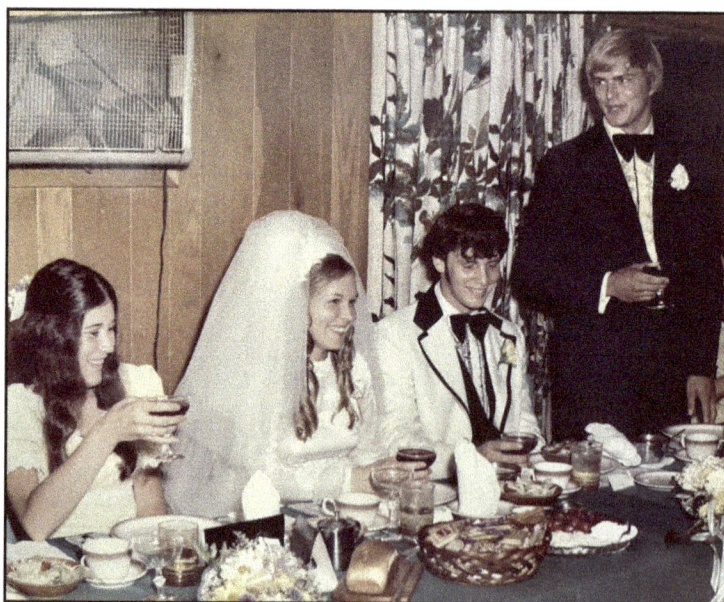

Head table at wedding dinner at Linden Terrace

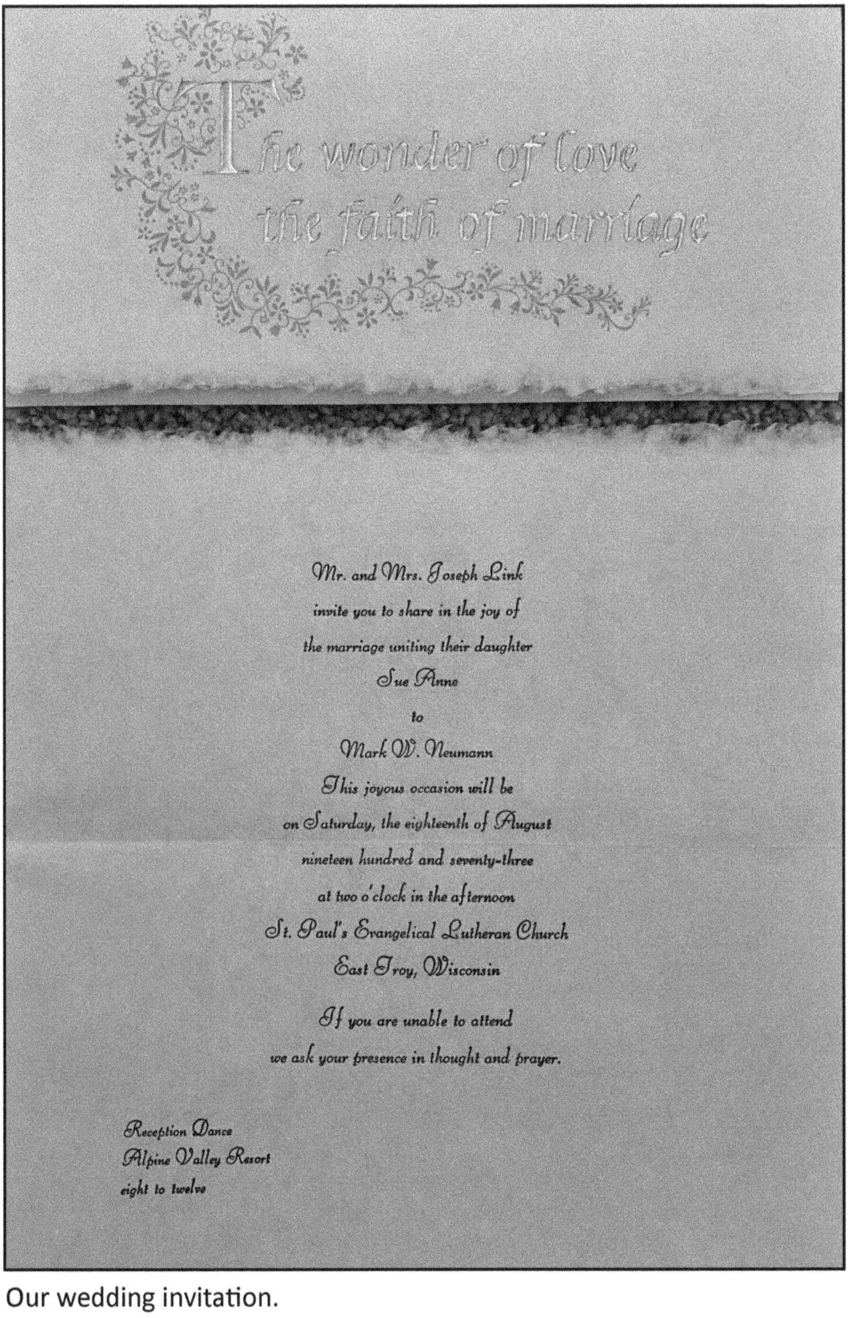

The wonder of love
the faith of marriage

Mr. and Mrs. Joseph Link
invite you to share in the joy of
the marriage uniting their daughter
Sue Anne
to
Mark W. Neumann
This joyous occasion will be
on Saturday, the eighteenth of August
nineteen hundred and seventy-three
at two o'clock in the afternoon
St. Paul's Evangelical Lutheran Church
East Troy, Wisconsin

If you are unable to attend
we ask your presence in thought and prayer.

Reception Dance
Alpine Valley Resort
eight to twelve

Our wedding invitation.

MARK *and* SUE

Our wedding church bulletin.

"I remember after the ceremony when we went outside, the sun came out. It was so beautiful. I was so glad we weren't going to have to take pictures outside in the rain."

Sue has a few copies of the lovely invitation left over, including some 8-cent-stamped return cards.

"My dad had wanted to see us drive away from the wedding in a fancy car," Sue said. "He went to the local car dealer in East Troy and explained the situation, that he'd like to borrow a fancy car for the afternoon. Back then you could do something like that. It was before limousines."

Just married! Mark and Sue with Mom and Dad Link and Mom and Dad Neumann.

Sue and Mark leaving the church in a Buick LeSabre Sue's dad borrowed for the day.

"What did he get?" Mark asked. "A Cadillac?"

It was a Buick LeSabre!

Mark and Sue invited friends to a dance at Alpine Valley after the wedding dinner at Linden Terrace, which couldn't accommodate the 350 people the families wanted to invite.

Mark was leery of anyone else fiddling with his car, so he hid it at Linden Terrace.

"I remember someone driving us back there," Sue said. "We had plates of wedding cake wrapped up in napkins to share with the workers who couldn't come to the wedding."

Mark and Sue spent their wedding night in Milwaukee, where Sue confessed, "Oh, my goodness, I'm starving. I only get

Mark and Sue cut
wedding cake at
Alpine Valley

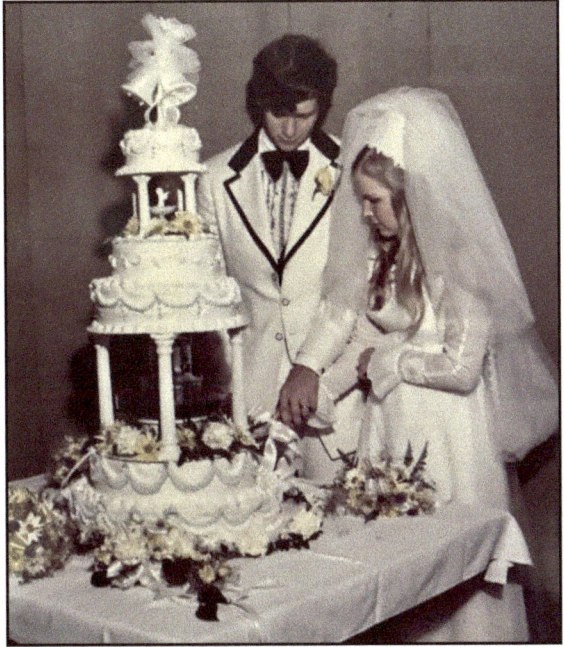

Mark and Sue dance
their first dance at
Alpine Valley

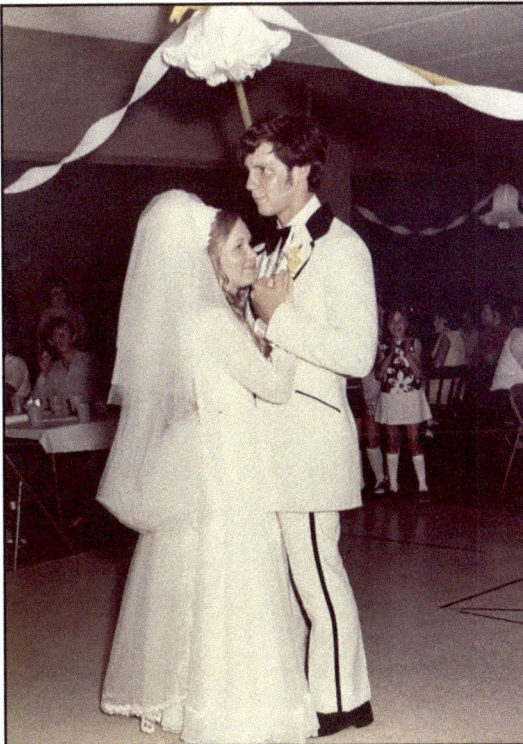

sick sometimes when I'm this hungry." She'd been so excited she hadn't eaten all day. "The wedding was something I'd looked forward to ever since I was a little girl."

It was 2 a.m. and restaurants were closed. "We had to raid a snack machine for junk food."

Early the next morning, they flew to Florida for their honeymoon. "Mark and I had never gone on a vacation," Sue said. "My parents never went on vacation because of the farm work. We didn't know how hot and humid it was in Florida. Also, the drinking age there was twenty-one, while it was eighteen in Wisconsin. The first time we ordered a glass of wine at a restaurant, they asked us for our IDs and told us we were underage."

Mark and Sue signed up for an official Honeymoon Program at Causeway Inns South. This program supposedly allowed them a twenty-four hour stay on the anniversary of their wedding through 2006—the next twenty-five years. The Special Honeymoon Package was eight days and seven nights for $247.50 per couple, which included breakfast, served in bed the first morning of their stay, Deluxe Dinners, a cocktail party, a dinner theater with a Broadway play, a trip to Disney World, flowers, and a full social program.

NEWLYWEDS

After the honeymoon, Mark and Sue lived in Whitewater while Mark finished his bachelor's degree, still working thirty to forty hours a week at Linden Terrace the rest of the summer and into the next school year. Since they owned one car, either Mark or Sue would bicycle to work or class. On the weekends, Sue would

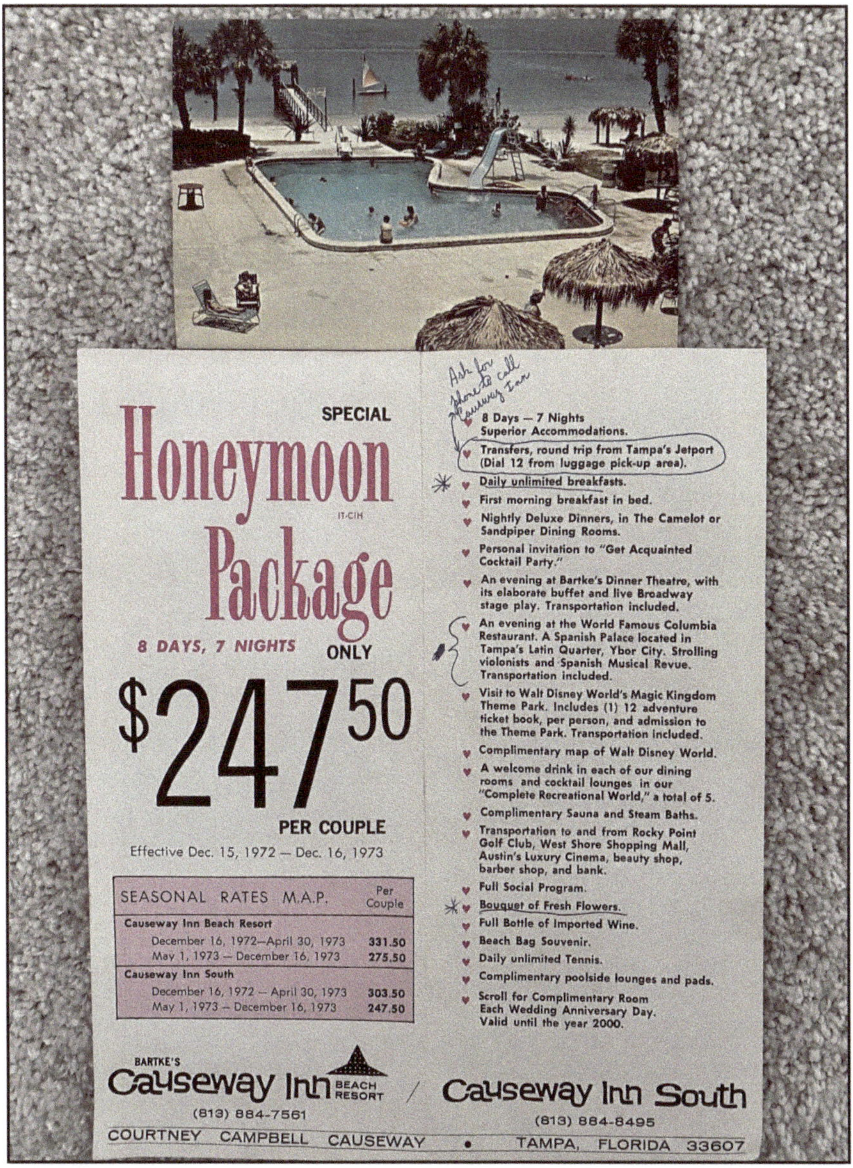

Honeymoon brochure and postcard, Tampa, Florida.

drop Mark off at Linden Terrace and drive on to spend the long days with her parents on the farm.

"I was married, but it felt like I still lived at home," she said. "I'd go shopping with Mom, or help around the house. I thought, I'm married and this is what it's going to be like: I'm never going to get to spend time with my husband. Weeknights that Mark worked were lonely, too."

"We got to spend time together in the car," Mark pointed out.

"It's not the same," Sue said.

Because Mark had the car for work or classes, Sue would walk to buy groceries after work. "I usually made two trips a week, at least, because I had to carry everything. It was just what we did."

Mark's UW-Whitewater transcript, 1975.

Mark was extremely motivated to finish his education and set a record pace, all while working full-time, refereeing sports, and learning how to be a husband. It was the latter that cost him his only B, for a 3.95 Grade Point Average semester. "I took an elective dance class at UW," he said sheepishly, "so Sue could come with me."

Dancing and Sue weren't the cause of the B grade, however. Mark missed a class to attend the funeral of Emil Hammerling, husband of Joan Hammerling of Linden Terrace, and his best friend Lee's father.

Both Mark and Sue recount those years as some of the best in memory. "We were crazy busy, but we were together, building our nest," Sue said. While she maintained contact with some of the close-knit friends she'd made in her technical school program, Mark recalls not making many friends in college. "I would go to see high school friends while we were here, but it wasn't the same."

"They weren't married," Sue said. "We were in a different place."

"Not into the drinking scene, like they were, starting in on beer at ten in the morning," Mark said. He was just too busy. "One semester I took so many credits, they couldn't put them on the report card." Those credits were counted as summer courses. He did take some credits one summer.

"We were on a strict budget and we just didn't have any money," Sue recalled. "Whatever money we had we saved and saved and saved for our home."

Mark's parents sent him a check for $300, but he returned it. "It didn't feel right," Mark said. "I gave up fully paid-for education at GMI to follow my heart and go to Whitewater to become a teacher. I got a school loan, but I put it in the bank to let the interest draw, then paid it off when I graduated."

To conserve their meager funds, Mark and Sue saved on rent by managing their apartment building. Sue worked full-time at Fairhaven Senior Care Center as a ward clerk while Mark finished school, taking a full-plus load of course work, and worked thirty to forty hours a week tending bar. "We could get a discount on rent as the managers," Sue said. They moved once after the first year when the building owner raised their rent $10. "We were angry," Sue said. "It was the principle of the thing."

"Managing the apartments allowed us to save for our own house," Mark said.

New table and chairs for our first apartment in Whitewater.

But there wasn't much money to pay for college and save, too. "The only thing new we bought was our kitchen table and chairs," Sue said. The other furniture for their apartment they borrowed or were given by family members, or bought used.

Sue typed Mark's college papers. "I was so nervous," she said. I was a good speller, while Mark was not. I wanted his papers to look good, and using corrector tape didn't look good if I made a mistake."

The two of them were so busy between long hours of school and work, they didn't spend much time together. "I thought after we were married I'd get to have time with my new husband, but I felt like I never saw him," Sue said. "I saw him more when we were dating. I remember Mark being gone all the time. We would drive to Linden Terrace to work, I would drop him off and spend the day at my parent's.

"Every weekend, I would bring a gallon jug I used to fill up with milk from the farm to drink during the week. It was another way to save money—we didn't have to buy milk at the store.

"Joan Hammerling was so wonderful and good to us. She would give us a lot of leftovers from the restaurant—leftover bread or meat or food from the buffet. We had great food— steaks and other things."

"It was awesome restaurant food," Mark said. "She would package leftovers from the buffet and let us take it home."

"She would pay us to scout other restaurants to see what they were doing," Sue said. "She told us she wanted us to check out the competition."

Years later, Mark and Sue realized it was her way to help us out. She knew we didn't have money to go out, and she didn't really care about the competition.

Mark looked at Sue with a big smile on his face. "You know, that reminds me of the ducks."

She grinned back. "I was just thinking the same thing. Mark used to like to hunt—still does—and he went out duck hunting one weekend and brought home four ducks. My family didn't hunt then, I was not raised by hunters—although now they do—so I had never fixed wild game. Someone told me I needed to soak the ducks in saltwater to take out the gamey taste, so I left them soak all day while I was at work. When I came home, the place stank. I didn't know they should have been soaking in the refrigerator. I learned my lesson."

All those years as Susie Homemaker—the nickname of the East Troy Future Homemakers of America club—didn't necessarily prepare Sue for real-world cooking. Aside from the duck incident, Sue recalled, "All my recipes were from my mom, meant to feed seven. It was hard figuring out how to cook for two. The first casserole I made was tuna noodle, which we ate for days. I didn't know Mark didn't care for noodles. He said I didn't need to make that again."

"No, I didn't," Mark said.

"Well, it was probably something like, 'you can make other things from now on.' We had a discussion about what I could make, and I learned he was a meat and potatoes guy, not noodles."

"No noodles," Mark agreed.

"My first washing machine was a small tub washer my grandma had," Sue recalled. "She went into assisted living and didn't need it, and so she gave it to me. It was the kind you attached to the kitchen sink, and filled up one side for the washing, and rinsed on the other side."

"There was a laundromat only a couple blocks away, but we were too cheap to go," Mark said.

He shook his head. "We were absolutely broke, studying, and working all the time, but they were still the good old days."

As part of the coursework to become a teacher, students have to complete some kind of student teaching or internship in a regular classroom. Mark chose to intern full-time for a semester.

"You got paid as an intern, which was different from student teaching," Mark said. "I got more classroom experience." It was a long ride from Whitewater back to Mukwonago, where Mark's cooperating teacher at Mukwonago Junior High School was Lois Sokolski. "She was a great lady, wonderful," Mark said.

Our first Christmas in Whitewater.

"She's still on our Christmas card list," Sue added.

"She had full control of her classroom," he remembered, "in a way you can't do today. She would kneel by the boys who were acting out and put her arm around them."

One experience during his internship changed his attitude about how to deal with students. "One child swore in my class," Mark said. "So I called her parents, and her mother's response included at least fifteen swear words. I learned to see where the kids came from."

The downside of the paid student internship was that the hours they could work outside the internship were limited so he and Sue quit managing the apartments.

"It was in college where I also learned about the mind working overnight. My favorite math teacher, Dr. Larry Davis, was a brilliant teacher who taught how we were to think, not just the core subject. He gave us a take-home test which we had to complete in forty-eight hours. I spent twenty-two of the forty-eight hours on that test, which was all proofs in geometry. I went to sleep, and when I woke up, I had the rest of the solutions figured out. That's how I learned that my mind can solve problems at night. It's proven a valuable asset over the years. Dozens of times, I would wake up at night with the solution to all kinds of problems, from subdivision and house designs to balancing the federal budget. That class was spectacular."

One of the many papers Sue typed for Mark was a report titled "Heat-Related Injuries – Diagnosis, Prevention, and Care," dated April 23, 1974. It was eight pages of careful research, obviously a serious topic for Mark who went on to coach high school for many years, even after he moved on from teaching. The paper received "Excellent" comments from his instructor, with full marks in levels of research, understandability, and readability.

* * * * *

Mark became a Wisconsin Interscholastic Athletic Association, or WIAA, referee that year, ostensibly to earn money, though Mark admits he adored practically anything to do with basketball. Refereeing for local high school games didn't even pay that much. "What was it, Honey, like thirty or forty dollars a game?" Sue tried to remember.

"It was twenty dollars, thank you very much," Mark said. "I enjoyed sports and it was a way to pick up some money. Junior varsity and varsity games paid a little more than freshman games."

Mark and Sue shared a conspiratorial grin. "My mom's sister, Aunt Sis," Sue said, "was very outspoken and opinionated. She thought we were way too young to get married."

"I was refereeing this basketball game, and I didn't have my wedding ring on," Mark said. "When you're catching a ball, you

Mark's WIAA basketball referee patches.

get swollen fingers, so I didn't want to have the ring on and have it get stuck."

"Aunt Sis came up to him and asked, 'Where is your ring?'" Sue said.

"I told her that I didn't wear it when I did athletic business. She told me I should never take my wedding ring off."

Mark continued to referee games, sans wedding ring, throughout their children's school years, though not for his own children's games.

Besides refereeing, coaching sports, particularly basketball, became so important he made it a prime part of his future teaching career job requirements. Mark kept the patches that had been sewn on the sleeves of his uniform shirt.

* * * * *

When graduation from the University of Wisconsin-Whitewater was eminent in the spring of 1975 and it came time to start applying for jobs, Sue typed the myriad of application letters, one by one, all by hand.

"This was before computers," Mark said. "We'd send out one letter at a time and wait for responses." Of the eighty-plus letters, Mark received several interviews. He wanted to coach sports, too, so that desire played a significant role in ultimately accepting an offer to teach high school math.

Mark spent two and a half years at the UW-Whitewater to finish his undergraduate degree in three years total. Several of his credits from General Motors transferred, and he took some summer courses one year. The practice of taking a full load of classes and summer school to graduate early became a family tradition. Mark and Sue's children finished their degrees a year earlier than typical.

Mark's commencement ceremony was held on May 10, 1975 at Warhawk Stadium, at 10 a.m. Mark graduated *magna cum laude*, high honors for having a grade point average between 3.75 and 3.9 in a 4.0 system, one of twenty-five graduates in his class to receive the honor.

"This time period of being so very broke is an important part of our story," Mark says.

Sue says, "We have to go through tough times to appreciate the good. We weren't born with silver spoons in our mouths."

Sue's dad gave Mark a special gift at graduation.

"Did you tell him to get it for me?" Mark asked.

"I don't think so," Sue said. "Maybe I mentioned it."

Mark's UW-Whitewater degree, 1975.

Mark and Sue,
graduation day,
Whitewater, May 1975.

Mark's graduation group picture. (L to R) Rob and Connie Germundson,
Mom and Dad Neumann, and Mark and Sue.

"It was a beautiful 12-gauge Remington semi-automatic shotgun," Mark said. "Buying it was beyond our means. It was the first time I had a shiny new gun."

"Do you still have it?" Sue asked.

"I think so…"

* * * * *

Years later, Mark returned to the University of Wisconsin-Whitewater to give a commencement address in his role as a Congressman. "The largest group I ever spoke to while in Congress was in Warhawk Stadium," he said. "I gave a talk that was very much me. College is very important. But there are things more important than higher education, like faith and family. To go forward in life, it's important to keep on learning…"

"But keep your priorities straight," Sue cut in.

"That's right, I said that," Mark replied.

"I told the graduates that faith and family were top priorities in life, even more important than education."

"I could see eyebrows being raised, professors in the front row whispering. I was never invited back."

"But you spoke at other college graduations," Sue said.

If Mark has any regrets about his college years at White-water, it was not playing college-level basketball. "I don't know if I was good enough for that," he said, "I never even tried out. I was married, working full time, studying, busy. I was a horse headed to the barn to get out of college."

RIVER FALLS YEARS, 1975-1977

One of Mark's personal requirements for taking a teaching job was that it had to include coaching sports, preferably high school sports, preferably varsity level, preferably basketball.

River Falls, Wisconsin, High School responded with a job opening that fall for the 1975-76 school year that seemed like a good fit. Mark and Sue decided to accept the new challenge despite being so far—six hours—from Sue's family.

With Mark's family relocated in Colorado, Mark and Sue thought they had all their ducks in a row. They moved to an apartment near school, in a building they managed, once again, to help save for a house of their own.

With a couple of weeks free, Mark and Sue took a vacation. "We flew to San Francisco to visit my oldest brother Jeff. He had quit school at UW-Madison and moved out to build picnic tables with his friends. He hadn't come back for our wedding and I hadn't seen him in two years. We stayed for a few days with him.

"Then we rented a car and drove to Los Angeles where Mark's older brother Dave and his wife Diane lived while Dave was in the Air Force. We did the tourist stuff like Hollywood. We decided to drive to Las Vegas...across the desert," Sue continued. "It was cheaper to rent a car without air conditioning and with a stick shift. What did we know? We drove across the desert. It was so hot we thought we'd die. At every gas station, we stopped and bought a bag of ice to sit on while we drove."

Mark and Sue stayed two days in Las Vegas then drove to Colorado to spend a few days with Mark's family. They camped. In tents. In the mountains.

Mark and Sue, 1975.

"I didn't care for it," Sue said. "It was cold, and then we slept on the tent floor, and washed in a freezing river." But they enjoyed family time before flying home.

* * * * *

When school started, Mark taught geometry, logic and reason, mostly to juniors. "Teaching logic is what I enjoyed the most. It was my best experience," he said. "I loved teaching juniors. They were a fun group of kids, not worried about college yet and just coming into their own."

But he didn't get the coaching positions offer in writing—another lesson learned. This was not the high school position he had been promised. Coaching sports, he learned, was freshman high school football, high school track, and junior high basketball.

"River Falls was a quaint little town," Sue said. "Nice. We didn't have charge cards back then, and once when I didn't have enough money at the grocery store, they said I could start an account and pay it off when I could."

Sue's work for the River Falls Nursing Home was quite different than at the Fairhaven in Whitewater. There, as ward clerk, Sue was in charge of purchasing needed items like sheets and blankets for the floor. In River Falls, she soon learned that all such items had to go through administration, the director of nursing to be exact.

"They said I couldn't order anything unless it was approved. I only stayed there six months. I didn't feel the job suited me and I applied across the street at River Falls Hospital."

At the hospital, Sue worked half time in medical records, typing reports, and half time in admitting. "They've built a new hospital out of town now," Sue said. "The old hospital on Main Street is now a Lutheran home."

Mark and Sue shared one car, and with Sue working full time at the River Falls Care Center as a ward clerk, they made adjustments. Sue would often drop Mark off and go to work, meeting him later at whatever event he happened to be coaching or refereeing.

"I really wanted to coach the same kids I taught," Mark said. His freshman football team had a 6-0 season. He coached eighth grade basketball. "We had a 7-3 year. The first game, I had this offensive pattern I taught the kids. They ran the pattern and ran the pattern and ran the pattern. I forgot to have them shoot the ball."

"Tell about the time you got kicked out of the gym," Sue said. "If you got three warning calls from the ref, you'd get kicked out. Mark was a little hot-headed—"

Mark's first 8th grade team.

"Energetic," Mark substituted. "It was the game where the brother of the starter at the other school was refereeing," Mark said. "I was upset about that. They called three fouls on three of my kids right away. I was so mad I hit my fist on the table." He took a second to catch his breath, reliving the moment. "I yelled at the ref and got kicked out of the gym."

"I walked in after work, later, and didn't see Mark," Sue said. "The seventh grade coach had stepped in. 'Where's Mark?' I asked."

"I was pretty upset."

"You were twenty-one years old," Sue said, "and you were on your own for the first time. You took it very seriously, standing up for your kids. When you do a job, you do it well. You learned your lesson and you never did it again."

"Right. I realized I had not set a very good example for my kids. In twenty-odd years of coaching, it never happened again."

"You learned to temper your emotions," Sue said.

"A useful tool during my Washington DC years," Mark said.

"Not really." Sue laughed. "You got kicked out again."

"That was not for temperament," Mark said. "It was for standing my ground."

* * * * *

Mark and Sue used the "envelope" system for household budgeting, storing cash in marked envelopes that would cover

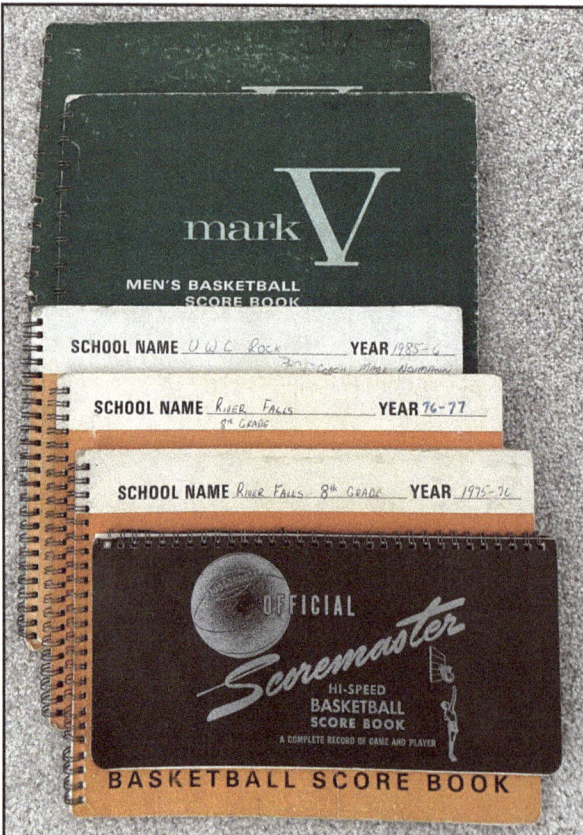

Basketball score books kept from all Mark's coaching years.

expenses and bills, such as gas, food, clothing, tithes, and an important one, savings. "If we disagreed on anything," Mark said, "it was that amount of money that went to the bank for savings, to save for a house."

Sue would sneak money out of an envelope on occasion. "Clothes," she said. "There was never enough money for clothes. The gas envelope would be empty and I'd get in trouble for it. But he was right," she said with pride and affection. "It worked out. We built our first house in River Falls when we were just twenty-two."

"We were so frugal in those years," Mark recalled.

Occasionally they would go out with friends, other teachers.

"Once we were at the local root beer joint, the A & W, and we argued over who owed the last ten cents on the bill. We were all the same," Mark said, "down to the penny."

"We had a lot of good friends," Sue recalled. "Other teachers. There was always a game and a get-together afterward at one of our houses. We'd go around to each other's houses and share snacks."

"Our friends would come over to our house with firewood for the fireplace," Mark said.

One teacher they still exchange Christmas cards with and still talk to is Jack Orgeman, a fellow math teacher who stayed in River Falls and retired from teaching.

River Falls is close to the Minnesota state line. Minneapolis/ St. Paul is only about forty-five minutes to an hour's drive. Once-a-month Saturday nights were often group pizza outings. "It was a trip to the big city," Sue said. "Rinaldi's. It was our favorite pizza place."

Mark and Sue were really only in River Falls one whole summer, in between the two years of teaching. That summer of 1976 was just as packed as the schoolyear. Mark taught archery and golf in summer school, while working on his master's degree, taking thirty credits, building a house, and managing the apartment building.

"You were always busy," Sue said. "Collecting rents, taking care of maintenance, vacuuming the hallways, running ads."

"We had to do it all, including rent the units," Mark said. "I remember the building owner yelling at me once for having an empty unit."

THE FIRST HOUSE

By living frugally and managing the apartment building, Mark and Sue were able to build a small house in the spring and summer of 1976. Lots of sweat equity went into that little green two-bedroom ranch house at 523 Johnson Street. Their backyard and garden were next to the small local airstrip.

"It was 1,040 square feet, with a one-car garage," Mark said. "We met with a builder in town who let us stain all the oak kitchen and bathroom cabinets and the trim." "It was a huge job," Sue said.

"Dad came back from Colorado to help us put a deck on the back and build a stone brick fireplace," Mark said. "I think it's still there," Sue said.

It is. Added to, enlarged, and still offering the best backyard in the neighborhood.

Mark and Sue also purchased their first dog, a yellow Labrador puppy they named Nugget. "We thought if we could keep a puppy alive, we could do okay with kids," Sue said.

Mark and Sue's first home, River Falls.

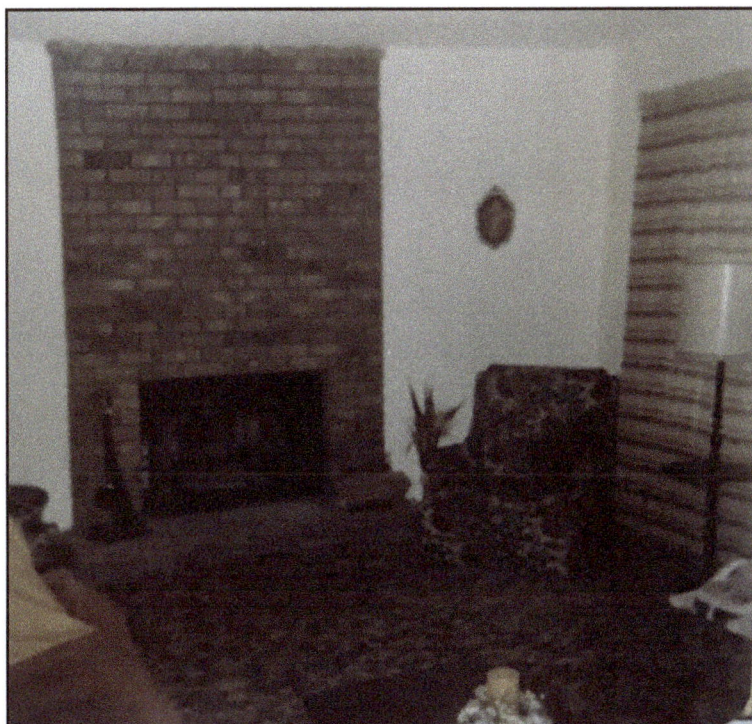

Brick fireplace Dad Neumann helped Mark build in River Falls.

"Nugget was a good dog," Mark said. They had her bred after they moved to Milton and kept one of her sons, King, who with Nugget were two great pheasant dogs.

"We did a lot of fun things together," Mark said. He took Nugget duck hunting on the Mississippi River. "The men would go hunting on weekends—pheasants and ducks on the Mississippi River, during deer season up to Luck, Wisconsin with another math teacher, one of my best friends. None of us had money then. We had no kids yet, but some of our friends had a child or two."

Mark and Sue joined the little Wisconsin Evangelical Lutheran Synod church in River Falls, Faith Evangelical. "It was a small little church on Apollo Road," Sue said. "We had a good group of friends there."

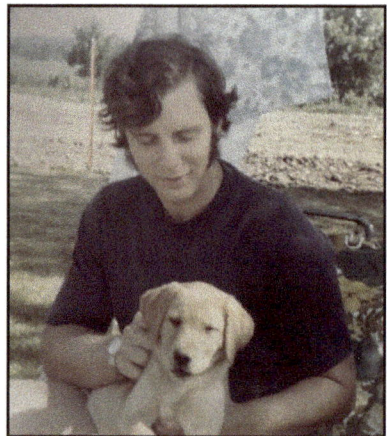

Sue and Mark with their first Golden Retriever puppy, Nugget.

HIGHER EDUCATION, TECHNOLOGY, AND SCHOOL DAYS

"We weren't busy enough," Sue said drily of their River Falls years. So, in the summer of 1976, Mark went back to school and earned his Master's of Science degree in Supervision and Instructional Leadership from the University of Wisconsin-River Falls while managing their apartment building, teaching, coaching three sports, and building their first house in River Falls.

"Dr. Jim Stewart was my academic advisor and instructional lead," Mark said. "I knew my life was laid out. I was a teacher, then I'd go on to become a principal, and eventually superintendent of schools. If someone told me back then we were going to do anything else we'd have laughed, we were so sure of our future."

Mark's master's thesis was about competency testing for high school graduations. What were the basic sets of skills expected for high school graduates across the state? He decided to survey schools all around the nation and ask about their competency requirements for graduation.

"It was the first experience we had in learning how to retype a letter on a computer," Mark said, "and change only the name and address. We did it at the college computer room." This was their first taste of technology to give them a competitive edge, a fundamental principle of learning how to apply technology to be more efficient. In time, Mark figured out how to use computer technology to advance their home-building business. "We had the first computers in the area for our businesses while the competition was still using hand tabulation to figure costs. At that time using technology to your advantage was a new concept."

* * * * *

At work, Mark had to deal with the same type of guff every teacher learns about. Children do not have a moratorium on bullying, something Mark and Sue realized then and later most brutally in the Congressional arena. "In every small town, there's a group who thinks they're in charge. I was always straightforward," Mark said. "No one got away with exceptions." And no parent's or child's excuses made him change his mind about classwork or grades. And there was pressure on Mark to change grades, both from powerful people in the community, and students pressuring their parents to ask him to do so. "The parents refused to believe this student was a problem and not doing the classroom work."

Mark drove a yellow Camaro before he and Sue had children. It was a favorite vehicle, recalled with great fondness as his pride and joy. His ownership was not a secret to his students, one of whom decided to egg the car during a football game.

"Did you ever find out who did it?" Sue asked.

"Yes, I did," Mark said. "Other kids saw and told."

Mr. Neumann's punishment was not to go out of his way to help the student in class. The car was stained until it was sold for the green woodie, a more "family" car.

Another incident is burned in Mark's memory. "There was this student of mine, a good kid, gifted athlete, attending a party. The police were called and the student panicked. He ran and jumped a row of bushes, right over a cliff, and died. I'm still sad to think about it."

"It's always sad times that shape you," Sue said.

* * * * *

Mark's first football team, undefeated.

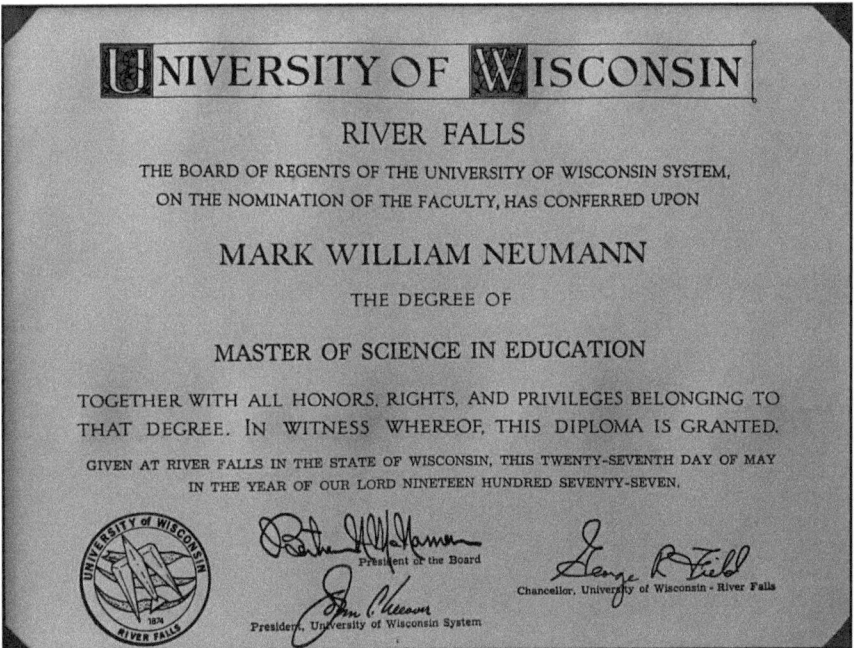

Mark's River Falls master's degree, 1977, with 4.0 GPA.

PARENTHOOD

Then came the year when it seemed everyone was expecting a baby.

"We hadn't exactly decided to start a family yet," Sue said of their second year in River Falls, even though many of their friends were in the family way. "It was a bit of a shock to learn we were expecting. I remember getting a bottle of wine and making a special dinner the night I told him. He was very excited."

"At least ten of our friends were all expecting at the same time," Mark recalled.

"I was last in line," Sue said. "We were a bit shy about being pregnant and hadn't announced it yet at this one party. All the pregnant ladies were sitting there, and I thought, *This is nice.*"

"Once, we decided to do something special for the girls," Mark said.

"We decided not to have baby showers for each other," Sue said. "Otherwise that's all we'd be doing."

"A group of guys decided to take our pregnant wives out to this opera in Minneapolis to celebrate."

"Are you sure it was the opera?" Sue asked.

"People had those glasses. Anyway, all the women were obviously showing." Mark grinned.

"All these people were looking at us, like, why are all these women pregnant?" Sue said. "Snooty people."

"The men decided to make a joke of it, and someone said, loudly, 'Isn't it nice, what we're doing? Treating these women from a halfway house to the opera.'"

* * * * *

Sue and her six of her pregnant friends.

Sue had been working at the tiny River Falls hospital. When Andrew Mark was born on April 5, 1977, there were no other babies there. "At that time, you stayed in the hospital after a birth. I was there five days. Since we were the only ones there, and Andy was the only baby in the nursery, I knew it was my baby whenever I heard a baby crying. I remember thinking that babies should never be allowed to cry and telling the nurse to get my baby."

The nurses thought Sue was uptight. "They told Mark to bring me a six-pack of beer," Sue said. "It will help her relax and bring on the milk."

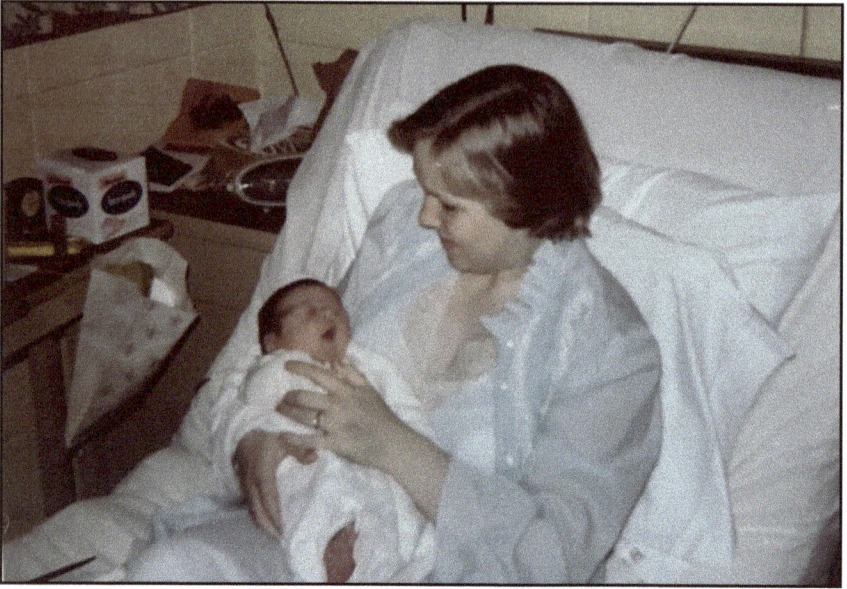

Andrew Mark Neumann born in River Falls (where Sue worked),
April 5, 1977.

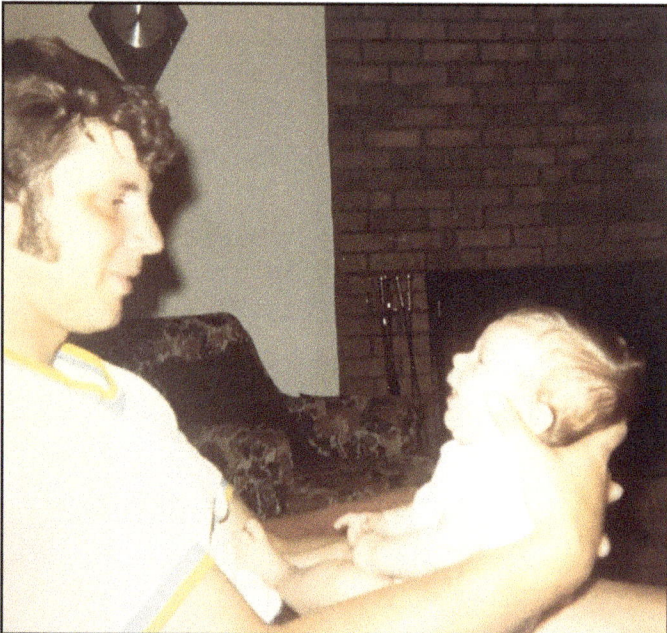

Mark and
Andy in our
River Falls
home.

When Mark and Sue brought Andy home, she would bounce him to sleep while sitting on the edge of the bed, part of the belief that babies shouldn't cry. By the time Tricia came along sixteen months later after the Neumann's had moved to Milton, Sue was informed babies crying was natural and she should put Tricia down for a nap or to sleep while the baby was still awake and let her cry.

"I wasn't sure how I was going to handle two babies so close together," Sue said.

They managed, and even had another baby, Matthew Kurt, four years later. Tricia and Matt were born at Mercy Hospital in Janesville while Mark was teaching in Milton, Tricia on September 12, 1978, and Matt on September 4, 1982.

But Sue and Mark had to get through a tragedy within their close-knit circle first. The two-month-old child of a friend got hung up in a swinging chair and suffocated when Andy was just two weeks old.

"When someone in your group dies, it's traumatic," Sue said. "I had nightmares for months, I was so shook up. I'd dream that Andy had fallen out of a window or had smothered in the laundry basket. I'd be digging through clothes in the laundry basket to find him. Mark had to wake me up and walk me into the nursery to see that Andy was all right."

A significant event prior to leaving River Falls was Andy's baptism. He was baptized at Faith Ev. Lutheran Church in River Falls.

Andy's baptism at three weeks. Faith Lutheran Church, River Falls. From L to R: Mark and Sue, Alan Link, and Kathy Neumann holding Andy.

FOR LOVE OF BASKETBALL

For two years, Mark taught math at River Falls High School, home of the Wildcats, but coached junior high basketball. "I wanted to coach the kids I taught," he said. "It's a different experience, going to tournaments. I wanted to step up to the next level."

He loved basketball nearly to distraction and desperately wanted to coach high school varsity basketball, which wasn't an option at River Falls. Despite coaching three sports, football, basketball, and track, and building their first home, the siren call of coaching basketball at the varsity level enticed Mark and Sue to move back to southeastern Wisconsin when Mark accepted a position to teach math and coach at Milton High School in 1977 to 1979.

"And we were six hours away from family," Sue added. "We wanted to be closer to home. It was hard on my folks. Because of the farm milking and feeding schedule, they couldn't come and stay with us."

Mark also had a job offer from Nebraska to consider. "Dr. Stewart arranged for me to be able to go to the University of Nebraska to study for a PhD in school administration."

"We prayed about it," Sue said. "It wasn't the right thing to do at the time."

"We are only the clay. He is the potter," Mark said, bringing his theme Bible verse from Isaiah 64:8 back into the picture. "We are the work of His hand."

First home in Milton, Wisconsin.

MOVE TO MILTON HIGH SCHOOL, 1977-1979

In those years, public school teachers were plentiful. There were more teachers seeking positions than jobs available. After sending out hundreds of letters of general application with the help of the computer to create a template instead of hand-typing individual ones, Mark was offered and accepted a position at Milton High School for the 1977-78 school year.

Sue's dad had always wanted to help them out. The news that his little girl was moving back close to home, he was going to do all he could to make sure they got there safely. "My dad took a couple of days in between morning and evening milking and drove around the area to find us a house in Milton."

"It was being built in a subdivision across from the high school," Mark said. "But we saw it and liked it, and bought it in time to pick out the carpet and the fireplace.

"It was the second time we chose a new home instead of buying an existing one."

"Mark could walk to school. Since we still only had one car, the location was perfect."

The house was only one way Dad Link got involved in Operation: Move Sue Home. "My dad called around to his farm friends and got a cattle truck lined up to help us move," Sue said. The move took place at the end of June and the first week of July. Mark, meanwhile, had gotten sick with pneumonia—sick enough for a hospital stay. But the old house had been sold and the Neumanns had to move.

"All of our friends and Dad's friends helped over the weekend. I had a three-month-old nursing baby and a sick husband, all while trying to pack. Then there was this smelly cattle car to move all our belongings."

They made a bed for Mark in the back of their green woodie station wagon so he could lie flat during the caravan down the pike. Sue drove herself, a new baby, and a sick husband down to Milton, with the cattle-truck load of furniture following.

* * * * *

Recovered and ready for the school year, Mark was assigned algebra, advanced algebra, and some beginning math classes. He was even able to implement a math competency test for high school graduation, as he'd developed in his master's thesis.

"I wanted to know what kids were supposed to know when they graduated from high school," Mark said.

He went out and surveyed business owners in Milton, asking what they wanted kids to know after graduation from high school. "What did they expect our high school graduates to know? The answers included how to make correct change and balance checkbooks, common-sense things like that."

Mark then wrote a test to see if the kids knew what the community expected.

The first time they tested the kids, there was an 80-percent failure rate. "The hotshot math department at Milton High sat back," Mark reflected. "We thought *'What's going on here?'*"

With the cooperation of the school board, Mark was instrumental in realigning the math curriculum and Milton realized a phenomenal turnaround in passing test scores during that time. Within three years, nearly all the kids passed. It was the motivation kids needed to do their work. If they didn't pass the competency test, they knew they had to go back to take the basic courses.

Mark coached freshman football. "It was a chance to learn a new system," Mark said. "We had good kids, and a winning 5-1

Milton Board Reviews Math Competency Plan

By BETSY LAUER
Gazette Correspondent

MILTON—The predominant subject at Tuesday night's school board meeting was mathematics. Senior high math instructor Mark Neumann presented information on the math competency program now in its second stage in the junior and senior high schools. In a matter unrelated to the competency program, a petition containing 33 signatures was presented to the board expressing dissatisfaction with the junior high math program.

The math competency program, which is gaining national popularity, is designed to show whether students are prepared to meet social math skills, Neumann explained. Fifty-eight percent of this year's junior class passed the test when it was given in October. This figure is better than average, he said.

The test is given in two parts and contains appproximately 150 questions, written at an eighth grade level. Students are asked to figure out problems relating to interest, discounts, adding multiple purchases and working with a checkbook.

Competency programs are designed to be worked into a school system over a period of years, Neumann said. This way, extra instruction can be provided for those who need it. At the Jan. 9 meeting, the board will vote on whether to hire an additional math teacher to teach 80 seniors next year who may be taking senior math.

The objective of such a program is to see that students do not leave the school system without meeting minimum math skills they will need in everyday life, Neumann said.

Students who failed the test the first semester of their junior year will have one chance per semester to pass the test. The board is considering making the passage of the test mandatory for graduation in the future.

The board is also considering testing the eighth grade math levels and revising the freshmen math program to meet the needs of the class.

School Board President Gailen Pierce presented the petition to the board. Two of the signers were present. The evaluation committee, headed by board member Jean McCartney will look into the issue. According to the petition, the parents are dissatisfied with the instructional materials and the system of rotating teachers. Dale Stark, junior high math department head, was asked by Pierce how many of these people had visited the class and had the entire program explained to them. None had, he said, and then indicated that the only visitor to the class since he made a course presentation to the board last fall was board member Robert Merriam.

Junior High Principal John Garvin pointed out after the meeting that of the 33 names on the petition, 20 families had students in the junior high and six of those received D-F slips this grading period.

Board Clerk Gene Wenham announced that Ronald H. Kaiser has filed a letter of intention to run for a seat on the school board in the spring election.

Dec. 20 was set for a long-range planning committee meeting to hear architect Jim Angus, Janesville, present plans to both remodel and reconstruct the current junior high facility. The meeting will be held in the junior high cafeteria at 7:30 p.m. The board, staff and public is invited.

A letter from Mrs. Carl Anderson was read by Pierce explaining how $1,010 was spent for a sign and flagpole memorial to her late husband, a former football coach. The flagpole will be dedicated next fall during football season.

Milton High School math competency test.

season. Our kids were so good, I pulled out our starters and substituted second and third-string players in one game when we were up something like 48 to 0. The assistant coach went ballistic because we had the chance at another shutout. He yelled at me from the sidelines. It was not fun to beat others so badly. Playing was all about sportsmanship, not how many shutouts we get a season. Annihilating another team is not right."

Mark and Sue again made close friends with other teachers. In fact, other athletic coaches for the school lived in their neighborhood. The after-game parties among the coaches and their families continued in Milton much as they had in River Falls.

"We'd take turns with pizzas and we'd all bring our own snacks," Sue said. "We had a nice network of friends. We'd get together to play card games. We babysat each other's kids. No one had any money, but the camaraderie was really nice."

"It wasn't all about money," Mark said. "There were great times. We got together and enjoyed each other's company."

Mark's salary was about $12,000 a year, even with the coaching. Although Sue returned to work only two shifts a week at Fairhaven, the schedule was difficult. "I worked PMs, three to eleven, as a ward clerk," Sue said. "I didn't want to leave Andy with a sitter, so I took him a few blocks to a friend's house for about three hours until Mark was finished coaching and could walk over to pick him up."

The friend was art teacher Sue Regez, the wife of head basketball coach Chuck. That cold winter, Mark would wear his big, heavy, winter coat, zip Andy up inside next to his heart, walk home, and make supper.

Mark's freshman football team, 1977.

Mark might have been okay at feeding babies, but the cloth diaper situation was not always his favorite chore to deal with. Disposable diapers were just not in the budget.

"I was pregnant with Tricia that winter, driving home a half hour from work, and I had to go to the bathroom so badly," Sue tattled. "I got home about midnight and both toilets had poopy diapers in them. When I came to bed, I told him, 'Honey, I think you forgot to take care of the poopy diapers.'"

"One of the only things we totally disagreed on was Tricia's name," Mark brought up.

Sue stood her place. "Our first baby had your first name for his middle name, and I wanted our daughter to have my first name as her middle name. I was looking through baby books and thought the name Tricia was so pretty. And it sounded better with Sue as a middle name rather than your choice."

Mark's choice? He started crooning the 1965 Beatles song, *Michelle*, by Paul McCartney and John Lennon.

"I still think Tricia Sue sounds better," Sue said.

"Happy wife, happy life," Mark replied.

Sue and Andy, 6 months.

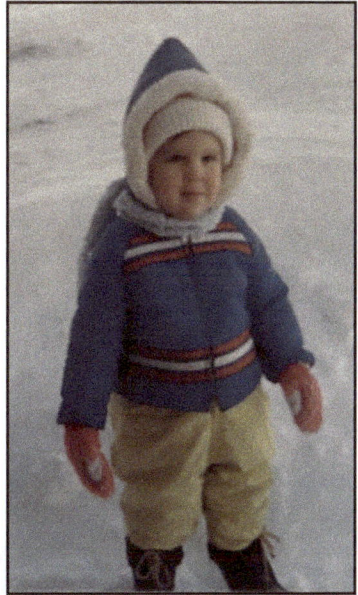

Andy in his snowsuit, 1 year.

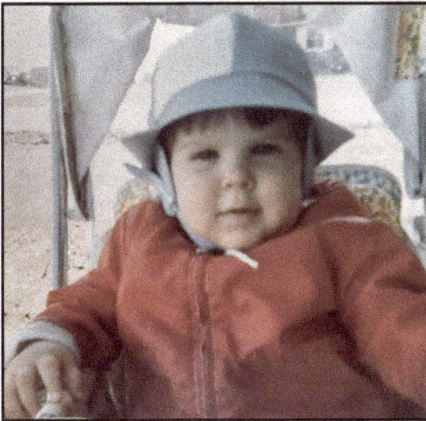

Andy in stroller, 1 year.

Mark and Andy, 1 year.

After Tricia was born in the fall of Mark's second year of teaching in 1978, with two young children to care for, Mark and Sue made a family decision that Sue would stay home and care for the kids. She did go back one shift a week for a short time during Andy and Tricia's toddler years until Matthew was born in 1982.

To save money, Mark and Sue bought cut-rate groceries at the local Copp's, which had the cheapest rates in town. Custom-

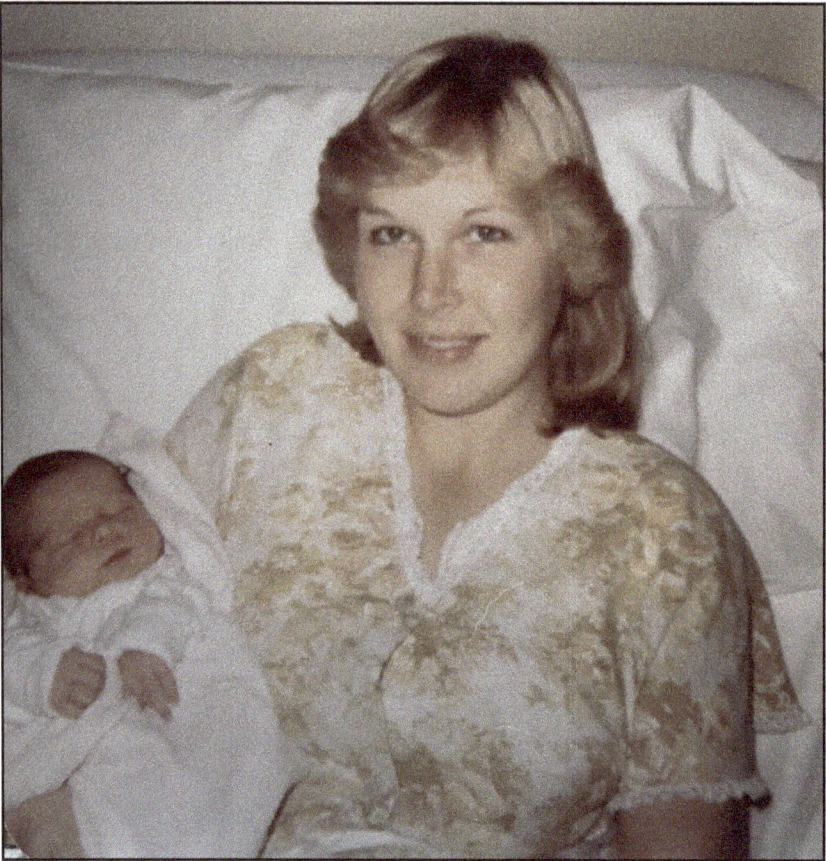

Sue with Tricia Sue Neumann, born September 12, 1978 in Mercy Hospital, Janesville, Wisconsin.

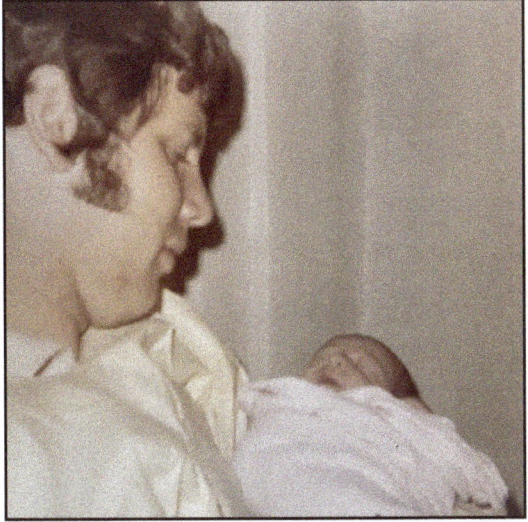

Mark holding Tricia at the hospital.

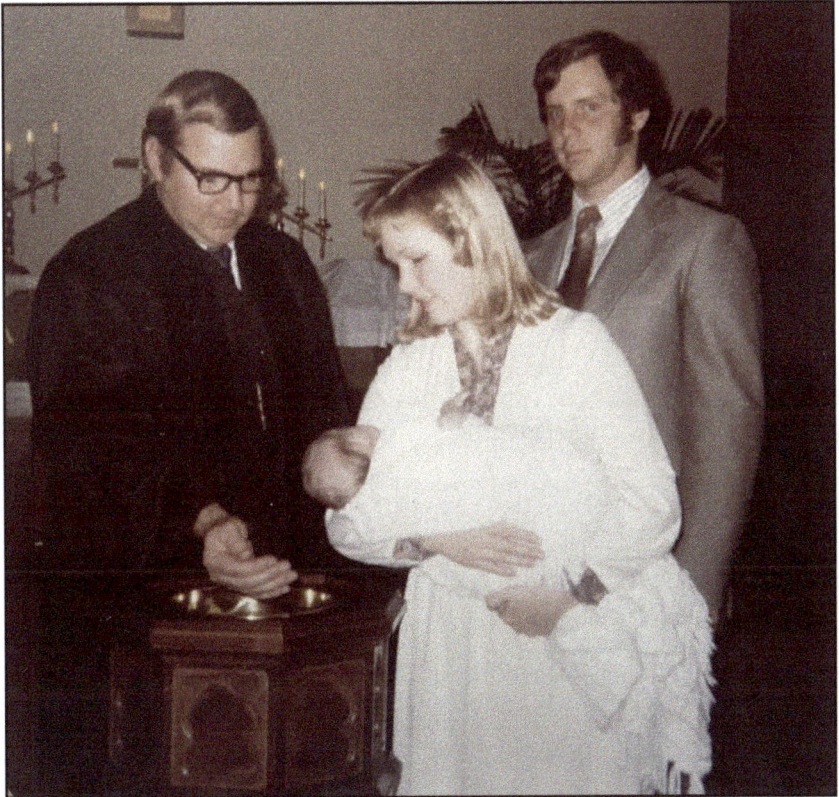

Tricia's baptism at 3 weeks, St. John's Lutheran Church, Milton, Wisconsin.

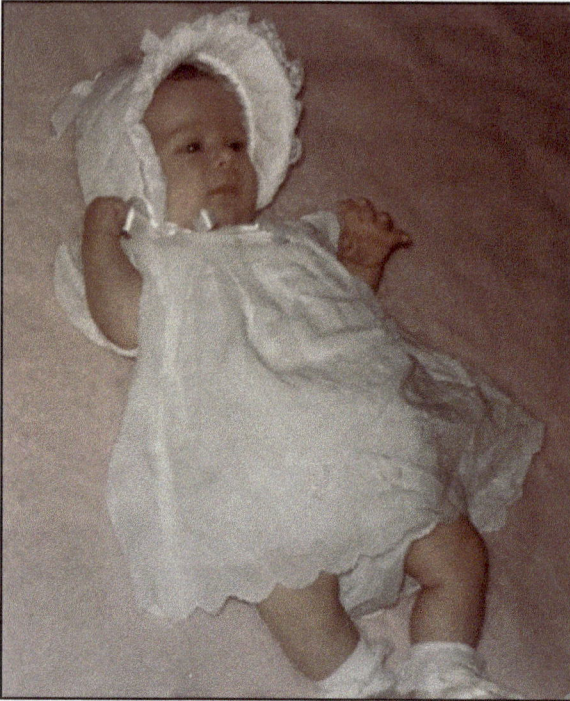

Tricia in the baptismal gown Sue had worn for her baptism.

ers had to price their own goods with a crayon based on the prices listed on the shelf.

"I remember one time when we had $28 to spend on groceries for the week," Sue shared. "I was pregnant with Tricia and craved cheese. Mark and I were shopping in Janesville, and I added a chunk of cheese to the cart. Mark was adding all this up with a calculator. At the checkout, we were over our budget by the amount of the chunk of cheese, and something had to go. Mark put it back, not knowing how much I wanted it. On the way home, I was teary-eyed. I told him I had craved that cheese—I was pregnant and wanted cheese. Mark felt really bad. Later, our daughter's first word was 'cheese.'"

"That was the good Lord dragging me kicking and scream-ing out of something I loved," Mark said. "This event was very influential in our decision to leave teaching and go into real estate. My best friend in teaching, Dan Pernat, who was about ten years older than us and the head wrestling and football coach at the high school, had a side business buying rental property, duplexes, for his retirement."

SIGNIFICANT DEVELOPMENTS

"Investing in real estate is a buy-and-hold or a buy-and-sell question," Mark said.

Mark considered Dan his mentor in directing the rest of their lives. They spent a lot of hours in the car on their way to and from hunting around the Wildcat Mountain State Park area. Their sons were about the same age and they got together a lot with the boys and hunted ducks, geese, and deer. "We'd get up and leave home sometimes at three in the morning, hunt around Wildcat Mountain, and come back at night," Mark said. "I received in-depth lessons from him regarding real estate investment," Mark said. "I started thinking about what Dan was doing. He was a buy-and-hold person and said to make sure the rent paid the bills. Then after fifteen years or so, the properties were paid off and one would keep the rent for income rather than making the bank payment.

"The first new theory I came up with depended on 10 percent inflation, which existed in the Carter administration," Mark said. "You can buy rental property with 100 percent borrowed money and the rents would pay all the expenses." The theory went like this: "So, if you bought a million dollars' worth of property, with 10 percent inflation, the next year your worth would be $1.1 million; within ten years you'd be a millionaire."

"But you have to be very disciplined to make that happen," Sue said. "It's not easy. You have to save and not spend it."

The theory only works with stable inflation. "That's too slow for me," Mark said.

"We found that if we were patient and looked around, we could find property worth more than the asking price because the sellers needed the money and wanted to sell right away. Here's our first example. We found a $30,000 property and bought it for $27,000. We put $3,000 down, so we owed $24,000 to the bank. We fixed up the property, got it back on the market, sold it for $30,000, and paid the bank $24,000. So we had doubled our investment and now had $6,000 from the sale to reinvest. The new theory was that if we could double our money nine times, we would have more than a million dollars."

Here's the proof:

- $3,000 doubled is $6,000

- $6,000 doubled is $12,000

- $12,000 doubled is $24,000

- $24,000 doubled is $48,000

- $48,000 doubled is $96,000

- $96,000 doubled is $192,000

- $192,000 doubled is $384,000

- $384,000 doubled is $768,000

- $768,000 doubled is $1,536,000

"I would regularly bet my students," Mark said, "that I could convince them they could become millionaires if they wanted...I won many sodas showing this principle. I would always start by asking them if they thought they could be millionaires and they'd generally say no. Then I asked them if they looked at twenty pieces of property, did they think they could find a piece of property for sale listed at less than it was worth...and we would go from there."

And that's literally what Mark and Sue did. They had saved $3,000 and bought their first property in the summer of 1978 for $27,000. The lot was on Elm Street in Milton and had two old, small, ranch homes, one in front of the other. Mark and Sue spent long hours scraping and painting the front house during the hot summer days, with Andy in a playpen under a tree in the yard. The other house was sided with old style asphalt shingles and needed some inside touch up.

In short, the painted house looked great and they sold the property, enabling Mark to use his mathematical acumen to figure out how to make real estate work without investing more than they had to spend.

The summer between the first and second year teaching at Milton saw Mark and Sue headed in two directions simultaneously. Mark enrolled at UW–Madison with the intention of obtaining his PhD. "We fully thought our future was teaching and school administration," Mark said.

He also somehow carved out the time in the late spring and early summer of 1978 to study for his real estate sales license, thinking sales would be a good side job for extra income. He took a part-time job with a local real estate agency, Webb Realty. He was under some pressure to get his own license, and had a couple of sales under his belt prior to obtaining his license, which were handled by the agency owners. He didn't keep the records, but a hunt from the Wisconsin Department of Safety and

Professional Services turned up the date of his first license: July 7, 1978.

Meanwhile, graduate school was an eye-opener. "In one of the UW courses, the professor called my master's degree a degree from Podunk U," Mark said. "I aced his course. In another class, I had two professors who were obviously living together, not married, and were fighting with each other. In shock, I dropped that one. A third class had a high-quality instructor where I wrote a paper on social security that I would later use while in Congress."

The crack in the well-planned future for the Neumanns occurred late in this summer when a decision had to be made to either show a house or study for an exam. Mark showed the house, realizing the PhD had to be put on hold.

"Looking back on this, I can again see the Lord's hand guiding and directing our lives in a new direction. We are the clay and He is the potter."

* * * * *

That summer between Mark's first and second year of teaching high school in Milton, Mark and Sue also decided they'd like to live in the country.

A number of reasons—from family to pets to social life—led to this thought.

Daughter Tricia was born shortly after the school year began in 1978. Mark coached the freshman football team that night after she was born, and his kids said nice things. "But, also, the varsity kids lined up and shook my hand and congratulated me," he said. "That was really special."

* * * * *

They'd bred their dog Nugget and sold her puppies—she'd had ten of them—for $75 each. "We had them in the basement during the winter and they made a mess," Sue said.

But another troubling social outlook crept into their young, faith-based, family life. "We started to not like the 'flavor' of what was going on," Sue said. "Small things were happening at parties like raunchy jokes, distasteful, off-color comments. Some of our friends were great. We didn't want to shun them or leave, but it was a strain."

"That isn't who we are," Sue said. "It wasn't something we wanted to be part of."

Andy and Nugget's puppies in the basement of the Milton home.

They bought a twelve-acre parcel of land on Jacobs Drive later that summer. The concept was to divide it into five lots, selling four and building on the fifth with a plan for the four sales to pay for all five lots. Jim Woodman, a surveyor, helped them out.

"It was our first experience subdividing," Sue said.

"I understood the math, but had no knowledge or understanding regarding subdividing property," Mark added. Jim Woodman became a trusted business partner with whom they worked a number of property acquisitions and divisions in the future.

The Milton city house Sue's dad had found for them was a typical 1,200-square-foot, two-car garage home. Their next house, the third one they built new, was 1,400 square feet with an exposed basement.

Jacob's Drive home in Milton, 1980.

"We decided to try solar power," Sue said. "It was a new thing and supposed to save money. We had panels on the roof. The heat from the solar energy was stored in drums of rock."

"Water would run over these rocks," Mark said, "to heat. It didn't work well, and it leaked. To stop the leak, we put eaves troughs in the attic and ran them outside. We eventually had to remove the system." He chuckled. "Now (2016) we own our own solar company, SunVest Solar Inc.—well, Matt does—and it's one of the fifty top solar companies in the country."

"That last year of teaching high school algebra in Milton, the spring semester of 1979, when I was showing kids how, with the current inflation rate, to become millionaires through investing, I made more money in six months working part-time in real estate than my annual teaching salary."

LEAP OF FAITH

Mark pulled out the Bible he kept at his desk and flipped through it. "This one is new," he said. "Sue got it for me for Christmas and it doesn't have the underlining and highlights from my other one."

He found the passage he was looking for in Isaiah, one he uses frequently when asked to speak, and a theme verse directing their lives. "Here—this, this is what drives us," he said. "Yet you, Lord, are our Father. We are the clay, you are the potter; we are all the work of your hand, Isaiah 64:8."

The Neumann plans and God's were different. The Neumann plans for a future in teaching and school administration ended and God's plan was implemented as Mark moved into real estate. Mark was candid about why he eventually left teaching public high school. "My first salary in River Falls was

$8,600 a year. We couldn't lead the lives we wanted without Sue's salary. And this was before kids. My salary at Milton was only a little better. It was either both of us work and have others babysit our kids or, if I went into real estate, I might make enough so Sue could stay home with the kids."

Mark resigned from teaching at Milton High School in 1979. "I was very nervous," Sue said. "We'd had a safe income and insurance with teaching, and now we had to rely on Mark's business."

"It was a risk," Mark said, "the biggest decision of our lives. We prayed a lot."

MAJOR LIFE-CHANGING EVENT—
LEAVING TEACHING HIGH SCHOOL,
1979

First Real Estate Lesson, 1979

Mark and Sue and the kids moved into their new house on Jacobs Drive that summer. After the monumental decision to leave the security of a regular paycheck and provided health insurance that came with his career in public education, Mark was hired as the office manager for a real estate chain in Janesville.

"It was a lesson that if I didn't sell, I didn't get paid," Mark said.

He was given a huge office in a brand-new building. "It was the biggest, most beautiful office I'd ever had or would have," Mark said. At that time, the company he went to work for was the twelfth largest real estate firm in the city. It eventually got up to number three.

"My job was to sell property, but also recruit agents," Mark said. The firm worked basically as a "rent-a-desk" operation with all the agents pitching in money to the branch owner for advertising and office expenses. Mark began to get requests for payment from vendors. Things were not adding up. "I was put into a position, as office manager, that I'd given my word to vendors who were not being paid by the owner. There were obvious financial problems, and because of that, my word was being compromised."

He and Sue shared a long look.

"I felt that what was going on was wrong," he said.

"We used to think, if this didn't work, he could go back to teaching," Sue said.

"I thought maybe it was time to go out on our own."

Mark put the finishing touches on the basement of their Milton home, creating a downstairs office. They laid carpeting, put in a drop ceiling to hide the rafters and ductwork, and set up a desk. Sue wallpapered the bathroom and decorated the new space. They bought new furniture and put in a cozy woodstove for heat.

MILTON AREA REALTY, INC., 1980-1986

On January 1, 1980, Mark and Sue opened Milton Area Realty, Inc. He was granted his real estate broker's license on January 7, 1980, which allowed him to act as an independent broker. Sue worked with Mark in the business as much as she needed to, and he needed her.

"None of it works without her," Mark said.

Sue admitted her special gift is in reading people, in greeting them and being a hostess. "I can tell if they're for real," she said. "I get a feeling about people right away when I meet them."

She may not be as uncoordinated as Mark claimed himself to be, but one of their favorite stories from the home office era came from a surprise entrance she made while carrying refreshments.

"I slipped at the top of the stairs," Sue said. "They were carpeted, and I fell all the way down while carrying a tray loaded with coffee and cups."

"Thank heavens she wasn't hurt," Mark said.

"I had coffee all up and down my slacks. I just picked myself up and apologized and got more coffee. Later, I had sore muscles. Those things happen." Sue chuckled.

The Neumanns not only had a pet dog, they also had a cat. There was a hole in the drop ceiling of the basement, where the cat had crawled up and gave birth to a batch of kittens. "We didn't go up there to remove the kittens," Sue said. "We figured she'd bring them down some time. But whenever she'd leave them to get food or use the litter box, they'd cry. You can imagine trying to type with these kittens crying from the ceiling."

"One time I was sitting at my desk with clients," Mark said. "Sue had brought us drinks, when this cat comes flying down from the ceiling onto the desk, knocking them over..." Mark shook his head.

Not so funny was the time the kids were sick. "I had two kids upstairs crying from ear infections while Mark had clients buying rental property," Sue said. "Instead of celebrating the sale, we had to take the kids to the emergency room."

Through all of this was the pressure to close a sale or not have the money to pay the bills.

FIRST OUTSIDE OFFICE

All of those little inconveniences of running a home business began to add up.

Within a year, Mark and Sue took the plunge to move his office from the basement of their home into Milton, not far from Milton College. They bought an old gas station and renovated it. Because of old gas tanks, they had to get the appropriate approvals and permits and clean up the site. The old tanks had to be removed. They remodeled the inside of the building themselves.

Former Milton Area Realty office in Milton, Wisconsin.

They hired staff for the real estate office, one of whom was Kathy Kittleson, a former student from one of Mark's university math courses. "She was one of those people who didn't know how talented she was. I got my first real lecture from her about not coming to work in flannels and jeans. It really set the stage of always being sure my employees felt the freedom to voice their opinions.

"We didn't have big cash reserves, but we needed an assistant and wanted to take on other agents to join us."

"Others?" Sue asked.

"My mom and dad," Mark said.

Kurt and Stella, who were in Colorado, were ready for a change. They had done some real estate business out there, but when Milton Area Realty took off and Mark and Sue needed help, Kurt and Stella moved back home to Wisconsin to help out.

Family photo: Mark, Sue, Andy, and Tricia, 1981.

Andy (4) hugging Tricia (3).

Mom and Dad Neumann with Tricia (3) and Andy (4).

Mark leaned back in his chair, eyes distant. "I'm not sure we understood how radically different life was going to be. If we didn't close a transaction, we didn't get paid."

On the other side, during this era of pre-Reagan tax rates, Mark realized that another downside of being in business for himself, was figuring out how many hours a week he was actually working. "We would reach a point that because of selling so many houses, we were pushed into the 70-percent income tax bracket and my motivation to keep working would be gone. Instead of making thirty cents to the dollar, I'd quit working in the fall and go pheasant hunting."

The first vacation the Neumanns took since leaving teaching was partly because of advances in technology.

"It was the first time I could go away because I could check my messages," Mark said. Using technology continued to make a difference in life and business.

"If you have people who want to buy a house, you have to stay on top of it," Sue said.

They went to a cabin up north. Getting away out in nature became a treasured tradition. They were also enamored with the idea of living on a lake and bought a vacant lot on Clear Lake, a spring-fed lake, in Milton. Mark and Sue obtained all the correct permits to put a road through the lot down to the lake and add a sand beach.

"That summer they had a massive algae bloom and people said we'd destroyed the lake. We got a marine biologist in who said we had nothing to do with it," Mark said.

Neumann family vacation up north, Wisconsin, 1982.

"It wasn't as much fun," Sue said. Weekend neighbors detracted from the family atmosphere that the Neumanns desired and they ended up selling the lot.

* * * * *

Sue reminded Mark they painted their own "For Sale" signs. They had the high school art teacher and former neighbor, Sue Regez, design their company logo and yard signs. They used a stencil and paint. The kids were too little at that time to help.

"One of the things real estate taught me was how to handle people," Mark said. "I'd start with the numbers. I qualified people for loans first, and would only show houses in their price range. Not everyone would do that." Mark's theory was that people could afford 38 percent of their gross income to cover all payments such as mortgage, charge cards, car payments, and "we could push it to forty." Of that, 28 percent would be what a person could afford for a house payment: PITI, or principle, interest, tax, insurance.

He pulled out the Amortization Book,

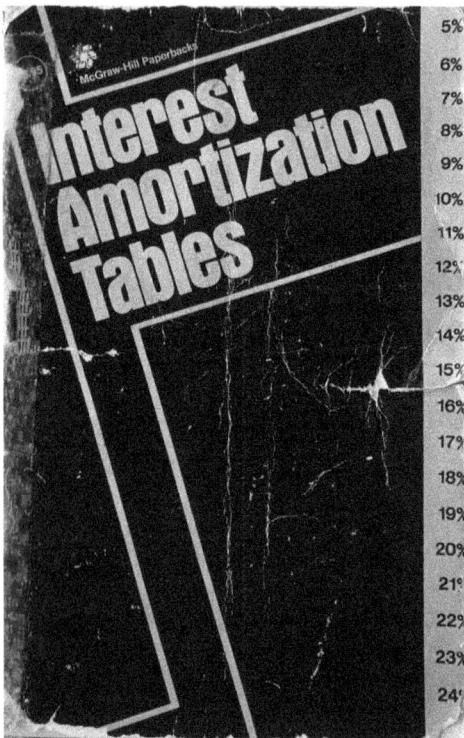

Mark's amortization tables used in the early 1980s before computers.

ragged cover and pages, to show. "I still use this," he said, rifling the pages.

"Once a new couple, teachers, were in town and I showed them some houses over the course of a day. Sue actually babysat for their newborn baby while we looked at houses. Some time later, they called me and said another agent showed them a particular house they wanted. I knew it was quite a bit out of their price range, but there wasn't anything I could do. Two years later, they came back to me in tears, ready to lose their house. I will not show people houses they cannot afford.

"We learned from Dan Pernat's example and our experience that a number of real estate strategies worked for us. I found God-given abilities that matched me pretty well.

"There are no guarantees in real estate," Mark said. "A couple of things happened that led us to become survivors. First in early 1980, the year we opened on our own for business, federal interest rates jumped from about 8 percent to 16 percent."

"It was scary," Sue said. "We had two babies and had left a safe job."

Second, the largest and another very big employer in the area, General Motors in Janesville and Dana Corporation, maker of vehicle parts near Edgerton, began to move the work force out of the area.

"GM decided to close down the plant and shifted jobs and workers to the Indiana plant," Mark said.

That meant 850 workers from Dana and "some 5,000 to 6,000 GM jobs," according to state Senator Judy Robson (D-Beloit).

Dana moved workers to plants in Milwaukee, Illinois, and Kentucky, eventually closing the Milwaukee plant in 2011, citing inability to compete with high wages.

"I was on my way to a closing when I received a call from the bank saying they'd canceled," Mark said. "They had heard about the Dana closing and since the home buyer worked at Dana, they weren't going through with the sale."

Between the two area major employers closing the local plants, "All of a sudden, all these people who had $50,000 ranch homes, on which they typically owed about $35,000, needed to unload them fast," Mark said.

Mark and Sue were able to jump in and pay many home-owners $45,000 for the homes they might have otherwise lost. "We'd rent some of them, but mostly would turn around and resell them, usually within six months or less, for $50,000. Most of those people were so happy we were helping them out. We'd earn commission on the sale, they'd leave town with between $5,000 and $7,000 instead of owing $35,000 and losing the home."

THE IMPORTANCE OF BEING AN OPTIMIST

During those years of the late 1980s, unemployment in the greater Janesville area hovered at 18 percent, according to the US Bureau of Labor Statistics. Because of the high interest rates, not as many people could afford costly loans to buy houses. The new construction industry was basically shut down.

"QuadGraphics, a large printer, was thinking about locating a plant in Edgerton. The representative got a speeding ticket when checking out the area, and they decided not to build here. We were told that nearly 20 percent of area residents weren't working and couldn't buy homes," Mark said. "Our theory was to go out and sell homes to the 80 percent who were working."

And here's the part where knowing and applying mathe-matical principles worked in a lot of people's favor. Mark and

Sue call it the "creative financing" principle. They were able to offer home buyers land contracts that would effectively lower the interest rate to a more affordable 12 percent.

"We used land contracts, mortgage assumptions, second mortgages, and anything else we could think of to move property," Mark said.

And, because the markets began to tank and real estate agents were leaving the business, that meant Milton Area Realty had less competition.

"It was all about the math," Mark said.

"If we could do creative financing, we could make it work," Sue said.

* * * * *

When Mark and Sue were able to buy their next property near Milton in late 1981, they purchased a large chunk of rural land, a 255-acre farm, but not before being turned down five times for a bank loan. They finally went to a local banker they knew, sat down and shared their plan. "He said yes," Mark said. "Our preferred business practice since then has been to do business with local bankers."

The farm came with a house and some good land. It was at County N and Vickerman Road, Sue remembered. Mark would take Andy and Nugget out there hunting. One time Nugget caught her foot in a trap. Someone had illegally set out small- game traps.

"It could have been Andy," Sue said.

The Neumanns rented out the old farmhouse and started selling parcels. "At that time and in that location, we could sell thirty-five acre parcels without any governmental approvals," Mark said.

Andy with pheasants
(5 years).

"There was a gravel pit on the farm, too," Sue said. "We sold gravel from it."

The other thing we did regularly on the farm was cutting wood. We had a maroon pick-up truck and Mark would cut and split a whole load of wood and sell it. Andy stood in the back of the truck stacking the wood as Mark did the cutting and splitting. We would sell the load of wood for $25, if I remember correctly, and for a treat, the family would go to McDonalds, happy to be able to afford it. In 1988, the last of the parcels from this major investment was sold and the project was a financial success, as well as a treasure of family memories.

EXTRACURRICULAR

Because Mark loved high school basketball so much, he continued to volunteer at Milton High School as the assistant coach under his friend Chuck Regez for the next three years. He was there coaching in the spring of 1982, the year the Redmen went to play in the Wisconsin Interscholastic Association State Tournament in Madison after a surprise upset against Milwaukee's Rufus King High School.

"Most didn't expect us to beat Rufus King," Mark said. "We were the underdog. Then we got slaughtered in the semifinals in the Red Barn at the state tourney in Madison, losing to Portage, 49-61."

Milton varsity basketball team. Mark was assistant coach.

Andy (5) and Tricia (3) at the state basketball tournament, 1982.

"The whole town was thrilled," Sue said. "They'd never gone to the state tournament before and everyone was excited."

Mark stayed in Madison with the team. Mark's parents came too. Sue was expecting another baby at that time, so she and the kids drove back and forth from home for the games. When she was cheering for their team, she said she felt so much kicking in vitro that early in her pregnancy—Matt was born in September—she knew he was a boy.

Mark and Sue continued their church activities. Mark played intramural basketball in school and church leagues occasional weeknights, but a lot of Sunday afternoons, going by the nickname "Roadblock." He shook his head. "I have no idea how I did all that back then. My son Andy went by 'Detour' during those intramural days."

One detour little Andy took is forever seared in his parents' memory.

"The kids—Andy was three and Tricia about a year old— were outside playing in the yard," Sue said. "I was at the kitchen sink, and checked them often through the window." On one of those checks, Andy was gone. "All of a sudden he wasn't there. I ran out there and yelled for him. I called Mark at the office and the neighbors to help look for him."

"We had ponds behind the house," Mark said. He and Sue feared the worst when Andy didn't respond to calls or show up.

"I remember running through the woods with Tricia on my hip. I was bawling. I had to find him," Sue said.

The neighbors were searching their yards, the road. Mark came home FAST. Once there, he noticed something. "Where's Nugget?" he asked. "Wherever the dog is, we'll find Andy."

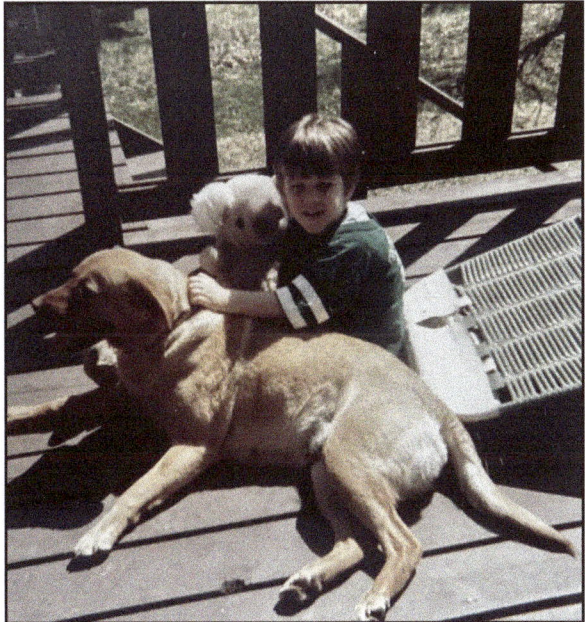

Andy and Nugget.

~ 155 ~

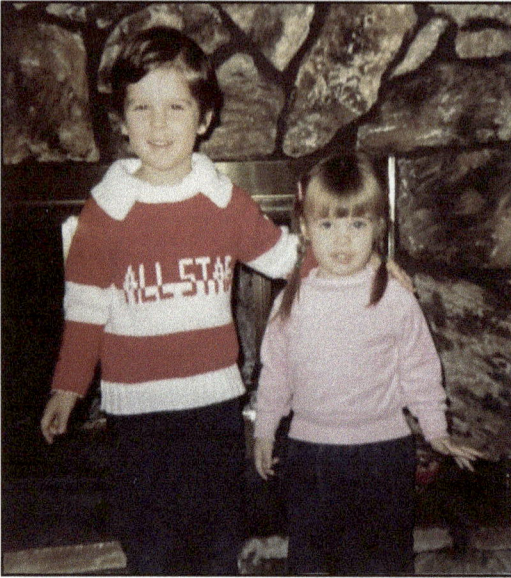

Andy (5) and Tricia (3), Jacob's Drive home, Milton, Wisconsin.

The search resumed with a new purpose. Mark began driving the roads, looking for Nugget and Andy, while Sue continued to walk.

"I drove to the end of our road and found him, sitting in the weeds," Mark said. He was crying, 'I don't know how to get home.' He'd wanted to take Nugget for a walk."

Andy and Nugget had gone maybe a third of a mile when he just wore out and sat down.

"The special thing was that the dog didn't leave him. Nugget just sat and waited," Sue said.

During this time Tricia, a toddler, and Andy were close buddies.

"She was a good baby," Sue said, "and worshiped her big brother Andy. He always watched out for her.

"Once when Tricia was sick, I took Andy to the grocery store while she stayed home with Mark. At the store there was a little girl who wore a coat exactly like Tricia's. Andy was sure it was

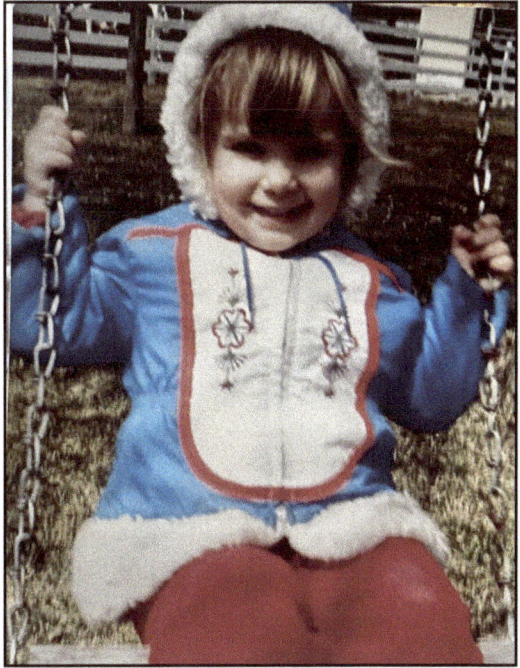

Tricia (3) in her blue coat.

her, although I reminded him that Tricia was at home with Daddy. He finally went up and touched the little girl's shoulder. 'Tush! Tush!' he said—that's what he called her. The little girl turned around. They were both shocked. Andy came running back to me. 'Not Tush!'"

MISSING TEACHING—MILTON COLLEGE, 1980-1982

"Mark said he missed teaching and the kids," Sue said. He looked around for another opportunity to teach math. Milton College, a small private school, had an opening for the fall semester of 1980.

He took the job—very little pay, but benefits—teaching some odds-and-ends courses with which he had little experience. "I recall teaching statistics, and I was maybe two weeks ahead of the kids, trying my very best.

"I remember one Christmas," Mark said, "when the class was taking finals. They were all looking at the charts in the back of their textbooks, which was allowed, but they were taking a lot of time." He began to walk among the desks. "They had written the formulas they were supposed to know for the test answers in there earlier, effectively cheating," he said. "I gave them all zeros on the test. It was a tough time for the kids who needed the credits for their degrees."

Most of the experience was good. He was still doing something he loved and was busier than ever.

"I remember I used to walk from teaching back to work at the office. We were writing real estate offers even at 10 or 11 at night. One time I was handwriting a contract around 11 p.m.—this was before computers—and I hadn't turned the carbons properly." Back in those days before copy machines and prevalent computer use, carbon paper was inserted between multiple sheets of typing paper to make duplicates. "So it had to be redone. I'd spent so much time with the details."

That year, Mark went from January into April without a day off. Back then they'd show houses morning, noon, or night, whenever people were available.

Despite all the activity, Mark started to feel a bit pudgy. He'd managed to put on about twenty extra pounds. "I could still play basketball," he said. "I was just slow. I couldn't even run to the end of our driveway. I decided I didn't want my kids to see me this way." He began a lifestyle change he maintains to this day. "I started working out, walking, jogging four to six miles a day, and lifting weights. For a while, Andy went with me, riding beside on his little bike."

"Until he wiped out," Sue said.

"He was five years old," Mark said. "And we'd started down this steep hill when Andy lost control and hit dirt."

A neighbor happened along and took father and son back in his car.

"I remember Mark carrying him in," Sue said. "Andy had skinned the whole side of his face, his entire cheek."

* * * * *

Matthew Kurt Neumann was born September 4, 1982 and life got busier with a full-energy baby number three.

Matt was baptized shortly thereafter at St. John's Lutheran Church in Milton.

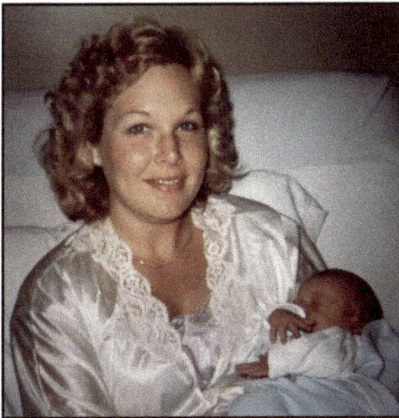

Matthew Kurt Neumann,
born September 4, 1982
at Mercy Hospital,
Janesville, Wisconsin.

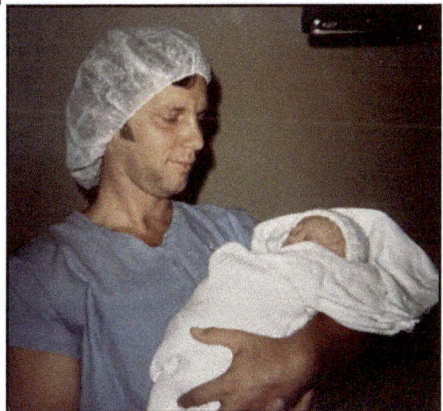

Matt's baptism at 3 weeks, St. John's Church, Milton. Mom and Dad Link (sponsors) and Mark and Sue, 1982.

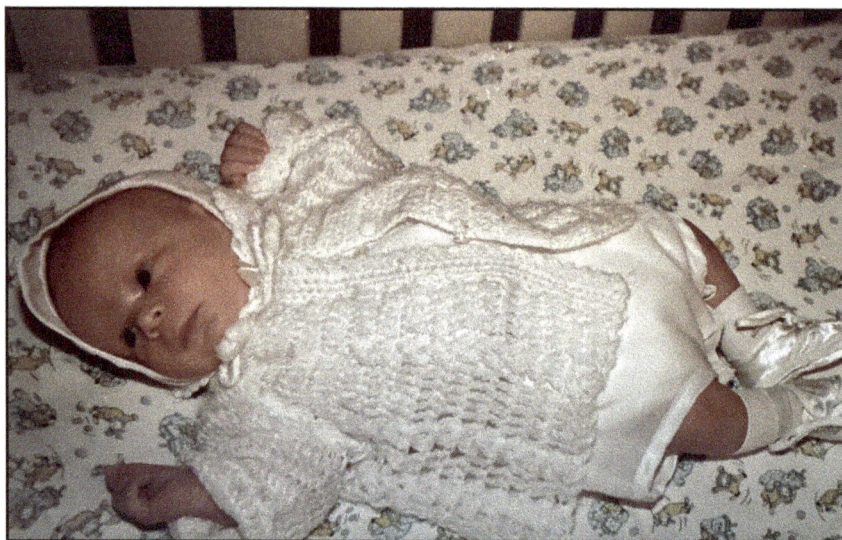

Matt's baptism, 1982.

U-ROCK YEARS, 1982–1986

In 1982, Mark and Sue were vacationing in Colorado with Mark's family when he received a surprise phone call from Milton College telling him to come and pack up his office. "I thought they were doing some cleaning or remodeling. They were closing down, just like that. Permanently. No warning, nothing. A lot of people were out of a job."

Many years later when Mark served on the Board of Regents for Wisconsin Lutheran College in Milwaukee, he learned that the library books and documents from Milton College had gone to WLC.

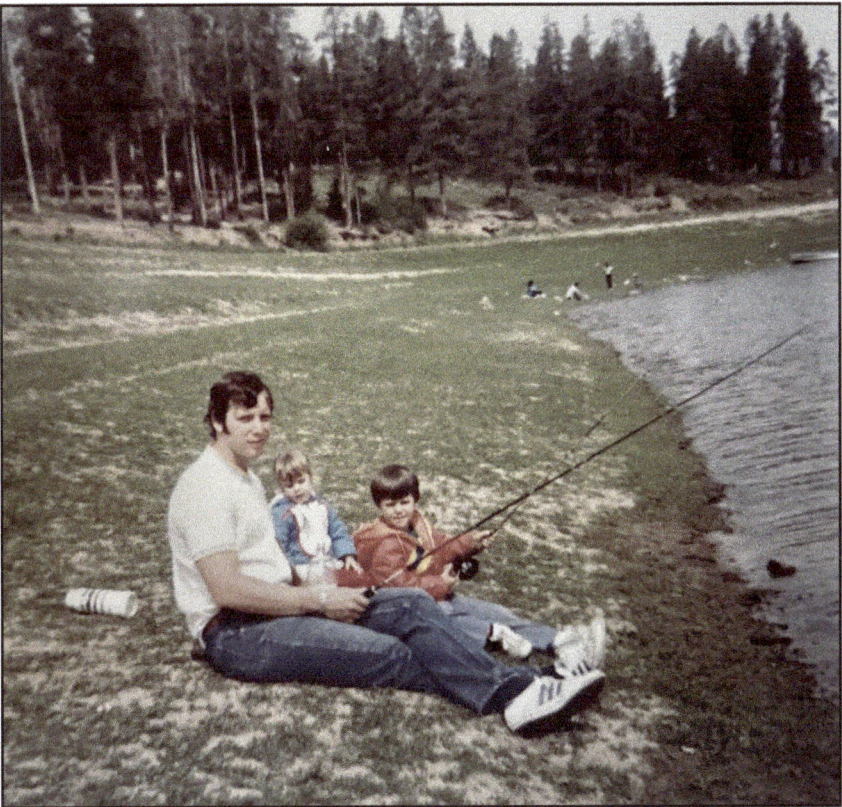

Colorado vacation, Mark, Andy (5) and Tricia (3).

Colorado vacation, Sue with Andy (5) and Tricia (3), 1982.

Mark soon found another position at a two-year college in Janesville, the University of Wisconsin–Rock County, affectionately known as U–Rock. For the next four years, until he and Sue decided to run for Congress, he taught up to four three-credit math classes per semester. "It was mostly for adults returning to school to get a degree, often people who detested math. I had to come up with something to make it palatable, so I taught real-world concepts."

Mark was also given the opportunity to start a basketball program. "They didn't have a men's basketball team." He got the program ready for the 1983-1984 season. They traveled with the college team to play other two-year schools. "We might get seventy-five in the stands," Mark said. To show how basketball permeated the family, Mark shared a story from a game with

Mark coaching the U-Rock college basketball team, 1984.

UW–Marathon County. "Our son Andy was seven years old, watching from the stands. We had three fouls on three starters early on, and I was stalling, trying to get to the end of the half, when Andy hollers, 'Dad, you can't stall, you're behind!' Everyone looked at him. We got the second half down by only ten points and caught up and won with the starters back in the game."

"The amazing thing to me looking back on all of this is that we managed to have over 100 closings in real estate during those same years, while teaching four 3-credit math courses, generally considered a full load, coaching, remaining active at church, and getting to all of the kids' activities and we had a new baby."

* * * * *

The closing of Milton College had other unexpected impacts on the Neumann family and again clearly shows God's hand in planning for their future.

"The college owned several parcels of land near our real estate office," Mark said, "which of course I was very familiar with. One parcel in particular had a lot of street frontage and I thought I could divide it into city lots and resell the lots at a significant profit. From 1983 to 1985, we acquired the parcel and subdivided into thirteen lots. It worked and we acquired an additional parcel of college land and put in our first street with sewer, water, curbs, and everything else involved in building infrastructure...with thirteen more lots. We called it Neumann Court."

Putting in the improvements, learning about right-of-ways, road widths, gutter, and sewer proved to be important. And again the direction of Mark and Sue's life was headed for change, this time from existing real estate sales into land development and home building.

Faith, Family, Raising Kids, 1980s and 1990s

Mark and Sue minced no words or sentiment when it came to matters of faith. "We were both baptized and raised Wisconsin Evangelical Lutheran Synod, or WELS, Lutheran," Mark said.

Both Mark and Sue were raised by parents who attended worship services with the family on a regular basis. They both retained that solid foundation and came to rely on it as a basis for their lives. The church's mission statement, "As men, women, and children united in faith and worship by the Word of God, the Wisconsin Evangelical Lutheran Synod exists to make disciples throughout the world for time and for eternity, using the gospel in Word and sacrament to win the lost for Christ and to nurture believers for lives of Christian service, all to the glory of God" isn't anything to quibble about. However, the doctrines and various isms of any church, any philosophy aren't going to be completely palatable to every member.

"If you start debating every point, there will be things we disagree with," Mark said. "[Church] is about your faith, not the body."

"By the grace of God, you're saved," Sue said. "No matter if all beliefs are right or wrong, we're forgiven."

This was where the passage from Isaiah had become so important in Mark and Sue's lives. "We are the work of His hands," Mark reiterated. "I don't have control of all the things that happen in my life. God has His plans."

Through Mark's speaking invitations, the Neumanns visited many churches. As they moved around the area, they visited various congregations, settling on Christ Evangelical Lutheran in Pewaukee. "It's a little more relaxed," Sue said.

Mom and Dad Link with Tricia (3) and Andy (5) at the farm.

Link family holiday dinner, 1982.

Another tradition in the Neumann family was family holiday dinners at the farm.

Summer visits to the farm were also made on a regular basis.

And of course, no Christmas was complete without a lacy dress for Tricia. This was always a special shopping trip for Mark and Tricia.

Back in Milton and Janesville, Sue used her musical gifts for the choir, and both Sue and Mark taught Sunday School and was a Bible Study teacher. In the early years of their marriage, Mark and Sue enjoyed devotions together, and later with the family.

Tricia (5) and the
Christmas dress she
shopped for with her dad.

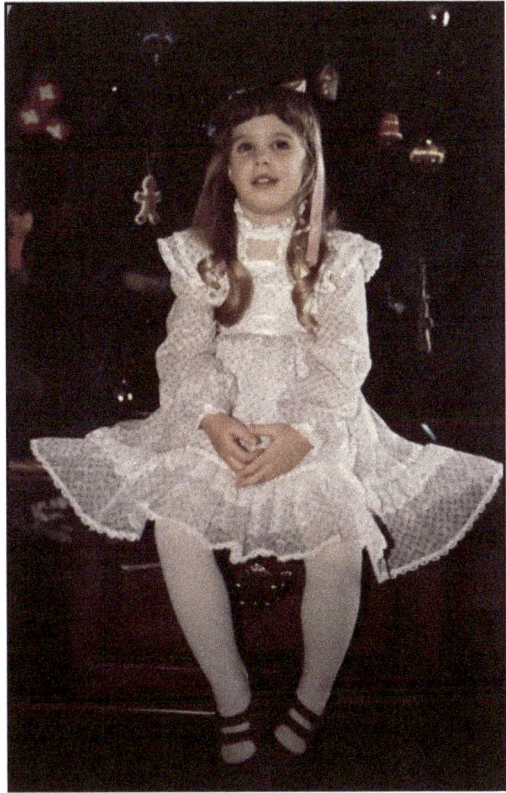

Mark has always been an early riser, up between 3 and 4 o'clock, throughout much of his career for private early morning devotions. Sue got up a little later, she said. The devotional time has played an important role in their lives and ultimately led to their leap into political life. Their favorite Bible passage comes from the middle of Jesus's Sermon on the Mount, Matthew 6:25-38, and His admonition, "Don't worry about your life."

"We used to worry about so many things," Sue said.

Mark added, "Things like whether mailed checks would clear the banks, pressure to make money, what others will say about you." Mark loves the book of James, and cites 1:3-4, "Because you know that the testing of your faith produces perseverance. Let perseverance finish its work so that you may be mature and complete, not lacking anything," as inspiration.

Mark was the first WELS Lutheran elected to the United States Congress.

FAMILY EDUCATION, 1982-1990S

Mark and Sue had some decisions to discuss and make when their three children began to reach school age.

"We'd both attended and were educated in the East Troy, WI school system," Mark said as the subject of educating their family came up. "We wanted our kids to have a smaller school experience."

The world had changed since Mark and Sue were in school. It was bigger, scarier, no more neighborhood schools, a lot less classroom control, a huge divide within freedom of speech and freedom of religion. Mark knew that firsthand from his years of teaching public school. "We wanted our kids to go to school where the name of Jesus was spoken every day," Mark said.

"Not just what we taught at home," Sue added. "It was a big decision. There were no Lutheran schools nearby, so we drove the kids into Janesville every day, to St. Matthews School, and picked them up from school."

"It might have seemed strange that a former public school teacher—"

"You were still teaching public school," Sue cut in. "And coaching."

"Oh, right, at U–Rock," Mark agreed. "Anyway, it might seem strange that we would choose to send our kids to private school, but we wanted them to hear about faith as a part of every course they took."

The twenty-minute drive had its advantages. "I would drive them in," Mark said. "It was a great conversation time with a captive audience. How many other kids spent that long talking to their parents every day?"

The tradition of daily conversation continued through Mark's congressional years, as they'd call and talk virtually every night when Mark was out of town. That two-way communication sustained the family. "In fact, I talked to them more when I was in DC."

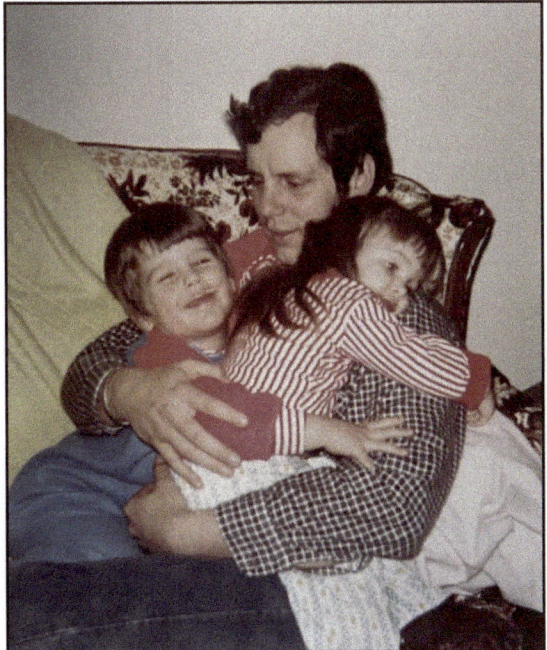

Mark getting hugs from Andy (5) and Tricia (3).

Mark, Sue, Andy (5), Tricia (3), and newborn Matt, Milton, Wisconsin, 1982.

Family Christmas. Andy (6), Tricia (5), Matt (1), Sue, and Mark, 1983.

Meanwhile, the family continued to attend church at St. John's Lutheran Church in Milton, active in choir and Sunday School and youth group as always. Sue said her wake-up call came when the kids sang in a school program. "The kids went to St. Matthews and had to sing at church. We were doing things with other St. Matthews parents, not our own church in Milton."

The youngest Neumann child, Matthew, started half-day kindergarten in 1988. The Neumanns were on the road a lot for school activities, from 1982 when Andy started school, pretty much until they all graduated from high school.

When Andy started ninth grade, the nearest WELS high school was Lakeside Lutheran in Lake Mills. "It was a forty-five minute drive from our house in the country on Jacobs Drive when we lived in Milton," Sue said. The kids were busy with baseball, basketball, soccer, cross-country.

Family time was a priority, and when the real estate business continued to grow and consume their time, Mark and Sue knew something had to change. Switching schools was not an option.

"We wanted Christ to be the center of their lives," Mark said simply. It was easier to make adjustments on the home front. Mark and Sue eventually made the decision to move to Janesville since the kids were already in school there. "It was better to live closer."

Andy, Milton Baseball.

Tricia, Milton Softball.

Matt, Milton Baseball.

ANOTHER CRAZY IDEA—
NEUMANN HOMES, INC., 1986 — 1990

"Here's another key to success," Mark said. He has a few different wordings to his pet theory, which goes something like this: "Surround yourself with qualified people who are smarter than you in your weakest areas and let them do their jobs. That's the part—get out of their way—that most leaders don't get."

In 1986, Mark and Sue let Kurt and Stella take over Milton Area Realty. "They were good at it," Mark said of his parents.

Mark and Sue started building and selling newly built homes as Neumann Homes, Inc. "Family Homes For Family Living" was the motto. "Our first year we lost $20,000 and my salary building nine homes," Mark said. "We were paying people by the hour to construct a house, and when you pay by

Mom Neumann holding Matt (4) in the Milton Area Realty office, 1986.

The Mark and Sue Neumann family, 1989.

the hour, they can drag out a project. It took six guys two weeks to frame a house. The second year, we realized that paying people by the job was much more efficient. When we paid by the job, it took three guys one week to frame a house, a 75-percent improvement."

During those first years, Mark used his yellow legal pad to run the numbers. Once again, Mark looked at the bigger picture.

In fact, Mark went back to UW–Whitewater and took a computer programming course to get a better understanding of how these new things worked. He wound up in a class with one of his former basketball players and they became friends. Mark also taught a class at UW–Whitewater during this semester.

"I remember distinctly bringing my stack of computer punch cards to the computer room," Mark said, "and dropping them off to be run through the computer, which filled an entire room while I taught the class. Things are sure different today!"

Home and business computers were starting to come into use, and he jumped at using technology to give the business an edge. "I'm a numbers guy," he repeated. He had a computer programmer come down from Madison to design a system of tracking the numbers and costs in the building process.

By the third year of business, the programs weren't designed to handle as much data as Mark needed to input, and they blew out the system. "We did not understand that computers had space limitations," Mark said. "As we grew from 27 homes built in year two of the home-building years to 81 year three, the computers crashed, causing major problems as it was not possible to do things by hand at that point. In hindsight, this growth from 27 homes in year two to 81 in year three, was not a reasonable thing to do."

Mark was also selling many of the homes that were being built but remained very committed to faith and family.

"We hired my brother Joe," Sue said.

"Right. We brought him in as construction manager. He heads the crews. Never be afraid to hire people smarter than you," Mark said in all seriousness.

The business was growing by leaps and bounds, up to 120 homes in year four, though that growth came with its own set of problems.

"Some people just don't respect your time," Mark said. Clients wouldn't make it on time to appointments while Mark scheduled his day around the kids' activities. He'd leave a sale

Outstanding Developments by an Outstanding Company

Year	# of Lots / # Sold	Name of Development		Location
1981-88	255 Acre Farm	Lima Township	SOLD OUT	Lima Township
1983-85	13/13	Rogers Street	SOLD OUT	Milton
1984-86	13/13	Prairie View Phase I	SOLD OUT	Milton
1986	5/5	James North Coop Development	SOLD OUT	Whitewater
1986	13/13	Neumann Estates Phase I	SOLD OUT	Whitewater
1986-88	14/12	Lakeside Acres Condominium		Whitewater
1987-88	15/12 15/13	Oakridge Forest Lake		Milton
1987-88	6/6	Pontiac Park Coop Development	SOLD OUT	Janesville
1988 January	8/8	Amhurst	SOLD OUT	Janesville
1988 April	22/6	Fox Hill Estates		Janesville
1988 May	10/5	Neumann Heights Coop Development		Fort Atkinson
1988 June	4/2	River Run Coop Development		Jefferson
1988 June	11/7	Prairie View Phase II		Milton
1988 August	13/1	Green Valley Estates		Janesville
1988 Sept.	27/4	Troyjen Subdivision Coop Development		East Troy
1988 October	4/2	Fox Hills Business Plaza Commercial Park		Janesville

1981-1988 projects developed by Neumann Homes (Mark).

on the floor if there was a choice between a late client and a soccer meet.

"The kids still today say that was important to them," Sue said. "We put in long hours in the business, and sometimes people could be rude, but our family was more important."

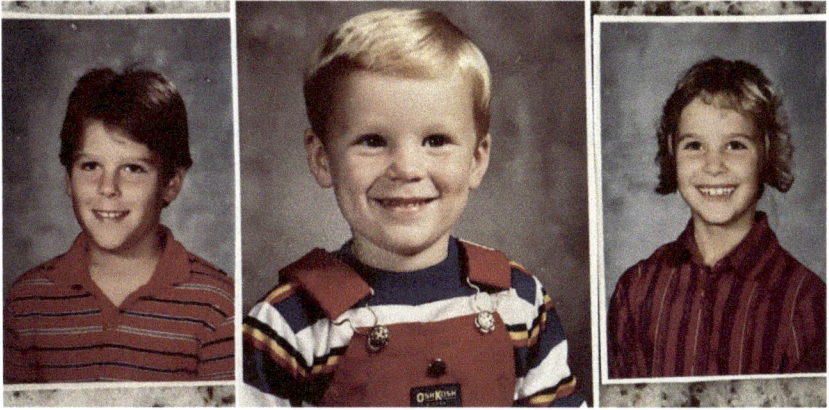

Andy (9), Matt (4), and Tricia (8), 1986.

Matt, Andy, and Tricia at the farm.

Besides the use of technology to speed up the pricing process over figuring a bid by hand, Mark needed another edge. "We had serious competition. We were nobody competing against big names. We started using quality materials, like real oak cabinets and trim in our houses, instead of the laminate and plastic others were using." But he didn't need to run his competitors down in order to show prospective buyers why they should buy a Neumann home.

"One of my sales pitches was that we bolted the sill plates in our houses to the foundation," Mark said. "Other houses are built so that the weight of the structure holds it to the foundation. I would show clients where the bolts were and ask the simple question if in a good windstorm they wanted their homes bolted down or to simply meet code and bank on that weight holding the home in place.

"So, you're building a new house, right? There are at least ten thousand components that could go wrong, like nails popping out of the wall. If your customer complains about ten to fifteen minor problems, the builder still has a 99.9 percent perfection rate. Most professions don't have a 99.9 percent perfection rate. We're competing against a customer's idea of perfection."

"People, especially those who've never built a house before, assume a new building is going to be perfect," Sue said. "We want them to know going in that it's not going to be like that, but that things can be fixed."

"There's so much money changing hands," Mark said. "It's easy to lose sight of how much went right."

The middle 1980s also saw the Neumanns grow their rental portfolio, part of the buy-and-own long-term strategy to realize a profit from investment property. "We bought many units," Mark said, "and had crossed sixty units at one point. Collecting rent was a complicated nightmare.

"I will never forget picking up a pregnant lady from one of our units to take her to the bank to cash her welfare check to pay the rent. On the way, I was feeling guilty and asked her how she was going to buy food for the next two weeks until the next welfare check came. Her classic answer was that her boyfriend, who was living with her, had his welfare check. I asked if he worked. She replied sometimes he rakes some leaves or something but that all gets paid in cash."

"Our worst experience was with the three eight-unit buildings we had acquired in Janesville," Mark said, besides an old house converted into six rental units.

"The three buildings were not subsidy housing, yet they were in a rough part of town," Sue said "Once Mark asked me in the summer when I was expecting Matt to collect rents. I drove down there. There were all these people just sitting there, not doing anything. Many looked angry. I came home after that and said, 'Honey, I can't do that anymore.' It was too scary."

One Sunday afternoon after Mark had been out to collect rents and was home, the telephone rang. He answered. On the other end, he was told, "I have a gun. I know where you live. Stop trying to collect rent. I'm not paying it, so stop asking."

One week later they sold that particular rental unit. Shortly after that, they turned the rest of the rental properties, some forty units, over to a management company.

* * * * *

Neumann Homes Inc. expanded into the surrounding communities, building homes and putting in subdivisions in Janesville, Milton, East Troy, Jefferson, Whitewater, and in Fort Atkinson.

Meanwhile, another lesson was about to happen. "We had purchased land and built Lakeside Acres Condos in Whitewater," Sue said, "just outside of an area of single-family houses."

"We got it all up and done and pretty well sold out," Mark said, "when we got into a dispute about—"

"Trees," Sue said. "People from the condos came back and said we hadn't put in the right kind of trees."

"I had documented everything. We were right. Our attorney said it was all good. He told us we were going to win the case, but here's what would happen. I would spend between $3,500 and $5,000 in legal fees to win $1,000 to $1,500. He advised us to just let it go and replace the trees.

"We learned to pick our battles. If you are going to fight a battle and win, make sure it's worth winning. Now, even if the customer is completely wrong but it cost less than $500 to fix the problem, we just do it."

The lesson was reinforced in a dispute with the city of Milton. In their first building project that involved street improvements, the city collected $75,000 from Neumann Homes up front and held it in a savings account that drew 12 percent to ensure they would do the work.

"They repaid the principle," Mark said, "but withheld the interest earned. I'd borrowed that money at 12 percent. We hired an attorney and went to arbitration.

"I'll never forget the day we were sitting in court. The judge looked down at us from the bench after reading the paperwork. 'I know what you attorneys charge,' he said. 'Your costs have now exceeded your potential winnings. So please leave. Case dismissed."

Hwy 26 Fox Hills Business Plaza that Mark built and also had his office.

26-unit apartment building in Fox Hills, Janesville, Wisconsin.

* * * * *

With the Milton Area Realty office in the good hands of Mark's parents, "We were ready to move the building business into our own building," Mark said. They opened up an office in a Janesville strip mall. Soon after, they wanted a more visible location and in 1988 bought property on the edge of Janesville on Highway 26.

Neumann Homes Inc. made plans to put up a substantial building, 36,000 square feet, with an exposed basement. They would have six units each on the first floor and the basement floor, some of which they'd rent out.

"Commercial building structural engineering is outside of my bailiwick," Mark said. He designed the building but hired an architect to draw the plans. "He made an almost fatal mistake." The architect failed to properly calculate the pressure against the exterior foundation walls.

"Almost as soon as we built, cracks began to appear in the basement walls," Mark said. "We could see the building from our house, and I remember waking up and looking outside every morning to see if our building was still standing."

"It's still there," Sue said.

They had to replace large sections of the foundation, adding additional support.

"Then, since we were so good at that," Mark said, "we decided to build a twenty-six-unit apartment building." Mark was asked if he wanted to act as general contractor for that project. "I recalled the pain of the office project and said no." They hired Roy Dieck, a commercial builder.

* * * * *

In 1988, Neumann Homes Inc. participated in its first South Central Wisconsin Builders Association's Parade of Homes in Janesville. The SCWBA, a 41-year-old organization at the time, had held annual home shows to showcase the products and services of its members. Mark's company built a home specifically for the show in the Fox Hills subdivision on Janesville's northeast side. The company had the lots divided and roads put in. Then they cleared the lots and built six homes and Mark promised his customers those homes would be in the Parade of Homes.

"Initially, there were no rules for how many homes you could show for the Parade of Homes. The rules were changed during the preparation of the show so that you could only have

The Fox Hills parade home, 1988, also our home, Janesville, Wisconsin.

two homes. We had six ready to go," Mark said. "It was my word to my customers against the new rule, and I chose keeping my word to my customers. The other realtors were angry, but we had them all ready so we had our own parade and spent more advertising it than the Builders Association. It was about keeping my word! We had a carnival atmosphere at our show house, with a hired clown and balloons and food. The other builders were upset and angry with us, but we sold a boatload of homes."

The Neumanns were called "clowns" by some builders for their tactics.

"We got over it," Mark said. "I have a great deal of respect for the Builders Association and after this unfortunate initial misunderstanding, we have worked together with the association and been an active member, even serving on the state board for many years."

Mark and Sue sold their Milton house and moved into a home in the subdivision in 1988.

While the builders finished home after home, Sue and Mark spent their Sunday afternoons at the new homes cleaning and staging them for sale by the 1 p.m. open house. The kids would come along and they'd have lunch together. Sue put up wallpaper under the chair rails in the dining areas, scraping off the sprayed-on sand coating first, and spruce up the bathrooms, adding little items like towels and bathmats in time for the open houses where prospective buyers could come and tour the house.

Cleaning and staging the houses was a job Sue could happily do, and have the kids with her. Office work—not so much. "I worked as an office assistant for a while…"

"She'd ask questions a lot—they were legitimate questions, but I usually couldn't slow down to answer them. One day, school called for her to pick up one of the kids," Mark said.

"I left," Sue said. "The kids come first."

"I said, 'But what about…' and she said, 'I'm out of here.'"

"He fired me," Sue said, tongue in cheek, laughing. "Again. It was more of a mutual decision since he agreed that the kids came first."

"The thing is, Sue had every right to ask as many questions as she wished and we both were committed to kids first," Mark said. "I did not always have time to stop and answer her and I too wanted the kids to come first."

* * * * *

After that first year of loss, 1986, Neumann Homes grew exponentially. In 1987, they built 27 homes, and the next year, 81. In 1990, they built 120 homes and the next year, *Inc. Magazine* listed the firm as one of the fastest growing companies in the U.S.

"All while doing land development in front of building houses, raising three kids, teaching, and coaching basketball, traveling all over the state. I'm tired just remembering that we did all that," Mark said.

As the company grew, the demand for capital was immense. "In those days, a check would take three to four days in the mail, and possibly another three to four days to clear the bank. I promised my employees their paychecks would never be late. I'd have a check in the mail to pay a subcontractor even if I hadn't been paid yet through a closing."

Mark counted on those sales. One example was a customer he'd built a house for in Elkhorn. The closing was set for Friday, and the clients decided not to close that day. "I had checks in the mail to my subcontractors. The clients had decided they were going to move in anyway over the weekend without closing the sale. Once someone moves in, it's hard to do anything about it," Mark said. "I had the house boarded up immediately so they couldn't move in. The clients decided to close and the checks to my subcontractors cleared the bank. I never bounced a check or missed a payday."

Besides rental property, the Neumanns were looking to diversify into other types of investment, specifically a fast-food franchise. "We were thinking of owning some restaurants," Sue said. "We were out looking at land to put the restaurants, but the good Lord was looking out for us."

About that time, the particular franchise they considered investing in wasn't doing so well. Mark and Sue dropped the idea.

In 1990, Mark's brother Ken had his own commercial construction business in Illinois. "The margins of profit on commercial building is extremely thin," Mark said, "about 2 percent, where the margins on home building is much better. We joined forces." That year, Mark received the "Entrepreneur of the Year" award from the University of Wisconsin–Whitewater for his business accolades. Later, Mark would sell the business in its entirety to Ken and use the proceeds to run for Congress

LOVE AFFAIR WITH HAWAII

In 1987, Mark and Sue took a special vacation that would come to play an important role in their lives. While the kids stayed with Joe and Laurie, Sue's brother and sister-in-law, Mark and Sue went to Maui with Sue's parents and stayed ten days. Joe and Beverly, Sue's dad and mom, had gone before and had fallen in love with the place. So did Mark and Sue.

"My parents had always wanted to go there on vacation," Sue said, "but couldn't because of the farm. They had been a couple of times and wanted to take us. We went to Honolulu, toured Pearl Harbor and tourist sites, and then went to their favorite island, Maui. We stayed there five days."

Mark and Sue bought their first condo on Maui, sight unseen, in 2002. When they needed cash to shore up the business in 2007, that condo had to be sold. "I was very sad," Sue said.

Mark and Sue's first trip to Maui with Mom and Dad Link, 1987.

"She never complained even one time," Mark said. "She said do what is needed to keep the business afloat."

"Mark said maybe we can buy another someday, and in 2013 on our 40th anniversary, he surprised me with one!"

LEISURE TIME 1982-1994

The Neumanns work hard, but also take time away for family vacations. Before one trip planned for Disney World during spring break in 1983, seven-month-old Matt had developed an ear infection. Sue's mom offered to keep Matt while the rest of them went on the trip.

"She was a nurse and said she would take care of him," Sue said. "I called home a couple of times every day to make sure he was fine. And he was."

Andy turned six years old on that trip. The pilot let him come up front during the flight. Later Andy was appointed to the Air Force Academy, but decided to go into education instead.

Andy with pilot on his 6th birthday, 1983.

Visiting with the Pernats on Lac La Belle, Oconomowoc, Wisconsin.

Other family getaways included simple hotel breaks, like one weekend to Milwaukee where the kids didn't sleep very well. "We were walking the hotel halls with cranky kids, and decided to just pack up and go home at 5 a.m.," Sue said. They also spent time with their friends the Pernats at their cabin on Lac La Belle.

In 1984, the Neumanns took a long three-week trip through the West.

"That was the Raindrops trip?" Mark asked.

"We sang all the time in the car to keep the kids busy," Sue said. "Raindrops Keep Falling on My Head."

They left right after school was out and drove their old brown van out to California. They put a mattress in the back for the kids. The first stop was San Francisco to spend a few days with Sue's brother Jeff. "We did the cable cars..."

Trip to Mount Rushmore, 1984.

"The Lake Tahoe stop was the most embarrassing moment of my life?" Mark asked.

"We don't need that in here," Sue said. "We went to Yellowstone, and drove back home on the northern route through Idaho."

Trip to California and Idaho, 1984.

Trip to Abe Lincoln's home, Springfield, Illinois, 1985.

Tricia (6), Matt (2), and Andy (7), Treasure Island, FL, 1985.

Another trip to St. Petersburg in Florida, Treasure Island and Busch Gardens, took place in the spring of 1985, and later, a summer trip to St. Louis and the Gateway Arch, with a swing through Springfield, Illinois and Abraham Lincoln's home site.

Andy and Tricia were in elementary school at St. Matthew's in Janesville and becoming active in sports—basketball. Mark had quit coaching the college team he'd helped develop at U–Rock and took on coaching a youth basketball team with his kids playing and their friends. They had a traveling team, playing in excess of fifty games a year. They played other schools in tournaments all over the area, mostly the state, but would also go into Iowa. Typically we'd spend seven weekends on the road in the winter season. The parents would go too and stay in hotels."

"Tell about Mark S. and the midgets," Sue urged.

"When Andy was in fourth grade, there were no boys to speak of in fifth, sixth, or seventh grade who could play basketball. There was this eighth grader, Mark S., a big, tall kid who was a good ball player. We had to bring up the fourth graders to play with him."

"They were short and fast," Sue said. "That's why we called the team 'Mark and the Midgets.'"

"Mark S. ended up with a contract to play professional baseball. He was a gifted athlete," Mark said.

Tricia also played basketball at St. Matthew's from fifth to eighth grade and was a cheerleader during those years as well. Sue helped coach the cheerleaders.

Tricia and fellow cheerleaders, St. Matthew's, Janesville, Wisconsin.

Tricia and the St. Matthew's basketball team, Janesville, Wisconsin.

As the Neumann kids grew older, there were more games and more competitive teams. Mark recalled a tournament in Iowa with Matt's basketball team. One of the players needed some motivation. "He was as good as anyone," Mark said. "I promised the team dinner at *Red Lobster* if they beat this ranked Michigan team, and he went wild on the court. The team won.

"Janesville Craig (High School) was always the team to beat," Mark said, memories of the years and boys and games all jumbling together. "I had put together a reasonable team one year. The Craig coach assumed we would lead with our usual highest scorers. Instead, I set Andy in the corner and he scored five times before they got a basket. We were up eighteen points

Mark coaching Andy's YMCA basketball team.

right away. The coach was so angry." The other team's clipboard was a casualty.

Another time Mark's team played in the Badger State Games and made it to the state tournament. It was so hot," Mark said. "That was before air conditioning."   "There were the final four teams before the championship game," Mark said. "The other two teams played first and we were in the second game. The team that won sat and watched us play. We won. The other team's coaches wanted us to turn around and play them immediately for the championship. They expected us to play again, like five minutes later.

"The parents of two of our players were lawyers," Mark said. "They went to argue with the officials that our team deserved a break. They lost the argument, but managed to drag out the talk for about a half an hour to forty-five minutes to give our kids a rest.

Mark coached Andy's Badger State basketball team.

"I never had a losing team."

Mark continued to play intramural basketball. He'd never stopped after high school, continuing to play during his college and teaching years, even during the congressional years, where there were no Democrats or Republicans but only Americans playing basketball. Most of his playing time was in the church league during the Janesville years, with other parents from St. Matthews. A memory surfaces: "In one game, I gave the principal a black eye," Mark said sheepishly. "It was an accident."

* * * * *

Mark coaching Matt's basketball team.

In 1987, the family visited Mark's brother Dave and his wife in Colorado Springs, Colorado, where they were invited to tour the Air Force Academy. It was also the year Mark went antelope hunting in New Mexico with a group of business people.

"I was not happy about that," Sue said. "It was five days away from me and the kids."

Mark went on the fall trip with his business partner, Ray Walton from Whitewater. What he didn't know was that a businesswoman accompanied the group of six. When one of the guys thought he'd try a little flirting, Mark never forgot her comeback: "I have a six-shooter and keep it under my pillow, and I know how to use it."

Mark on New Mexico antelope hunting trip, 1987.

"It was on that trip I learned about women and guns. I'd never heard anyone call a gun a six-shooter before," he said. "She could take care of herself."

Another vacation to Florida in 1988 included a long, long, long drive down to Key West. "Friends told us we should see it, so we decided to go," Sue said. "We got all the way down there, took one picture, then drove back. We thought, *What did we come down here for?*"

In the fall of that year, Sue's dad turned 65 and he "kinda retired." He sold the dairy to his sons, but kept working in the fields. The family came together for a birthday party for Sue's dad.

Each of the three Neumann kids spent a three-night stay on the farm while they were growing up. "It was one-on-one time with Grandma and Grandpa," Sue said.

Mom and Dad Link, 65th birthday at our home in Fox Hills, Janesville, Wisconsin, 1988.

Tricia shared her mother's love affair with kittens. "She started getting kitties," Sue said. "She wanted a kitty and Daddy would go get kitties." It wasn't only kitties Tricia's daddy would get for her.

Each year Mark and Tricia had a Daddy-Daughter date to pick out a Christmas dress. Not just any dress, but the prettiest, frilliest dress of Tricia's heart.

Tricia in beautiful Christmas dresses shopped for with Dad.

Mark with moose horns, British Columbia, Canada, 2002.

Mark continued the family hunting and fishing tradition with the kids. He's gone elk hunting in Colorado several times, and moose hunting in British Columbia, Canada. "Since we lived on Moose Lake at the time, Sue said we needed some moose horns over this fireplace." He was able to supply the horns in 2002.

Mark had hunted deer, turkey, pheasant, and ducks. While elk hunting with his sons, he remembered son Andy dragging him up this mountain in Colorado in the fall of 1988, even though Mark said he had to talk Andy into going on the trip. "We argue to this day who shot the biggest one."

From a young age, hunting with his father to later hunting with his own boys and grandsons, hunting has been an important family tradition building strong bonds. Hunting is a Neumann Family tradition.

The hunting gene has been passed on to the next generation. Son Matthew's oldest boy, Max, let his teacher know what really happens with turkeys. "His kindergarten teacher shows pictures of turkeys to the class and asked them 'What do we do with turkeys?' Max said we shoot and eat them.'"

Almost every summer since the kids were in school, the Neumanns have gone to remote camps in Canada for fishing. Mark's parents have gone, too.

Hunting . . . "A Neumann Family Tradition"

Elk-hunting trip, Mark and Dad Neumann, 1988.

Andy, Mark, and Matt. Elk hunt 2003; all were successful.

Annual Canada trip. Mark, Sue, Andy, Tricia, Matt, and Mom and Dad Neumann.

It used to be a male-bonding ritual until the year daughter Tricia turned sixteen and got her driver's license in 1993. A little accident with the car sliding into a curve and doing a couple of thousand dollars' worth of damage to the underside would have been cause enough for concern, but Tricia failed to mention it, then tried to deny it. When she fessed up, her dad gave her two choices. She could work for him all summer to pay him back for the cost of repairs, or she could go up to Canada for the five-day trip with all boys, including uncles and cousins, no phones, mirrors or indoor plumbing. She chose the five-day purgatory.

"We had just landed," Mark said, "after flying in. Matt and Tricia and I were in a boat, I was driving. Tricia was in the middle, and Matt in front. I threw a line in and tied into what I knew was a big fish, bigger than my test line. I told Matt to come back and drive the boat, so Matt comes to the back and Tricia moves to the front." Meanwhile, Mark holds the fishing pole, directing Matt to keep driving after the fish so as not to lose it.

The fish began to tire and Mark directed Tricia to get the net. "Tricia takes a swing at it, literally, with the net. This went on forever. Finally, the fish was completely tired out and we were able to bring it in." It was a huge northern which they mounted. A favorite framed photo Mark keeps in his office is a gift from his daughter posing with a stringer of fish.

"When she came home," Sue said, "she told me I had to go the next time. It was so much fun."

Sue reluctantly agreed. "Since then, the women have gone along," Sue said. Though now they need a place with indoor plumbing after the bear incident.

"I was in the outhouse on one trip," Mark said, when I heard them yelling at me not to come out because there was a bear. I thought they were kidding, so I came out. There was a bear."

Mark with a large Northern Pike,
Canada, 1993.

Mark and Tricia with Northern
Pikes, Canada trip, 1993.

Mom Neumann, Stella, in her special recliner. Canada fishing trip with great-grandsons Will, Charlie, and Oliver Neumann, 2019.

Mom Neumann in her 80s; Canada fishing trip.

"Mark's mom said that if Sue was going, she would come too," Sue said. Stella still enjoyed the trip into her eighties. In her later years, they even flew in a recliner for her so she would keep coming.

THE TURNING POINT—
FAMILY VACATION TO WASHINGTON DC, 1989

When deciding where to take a family vacation in 1989, Mark wanted to go up North fishing. "I told him we should take the kids someplace else we've never been. Somewhere educational, maybe a history lesson.

"I should have never, ever said that," Sue said. "We'd never been political, other than voting," Sue said. "We'd never even donated to a political party. We were busy with our business, church, and family. It was my hare-brained idea to see our nation's capital."

"Sue said it," Mark added. "It was her idea. The DC trip in 1989 is where the good Lord led us to change our minds. We are the clay, and He is the potter."

The family loaded up the van and left after school was out in late May. They'd planned a nine-day trip, two days to see Washington DC, then go to New York City, and on to other sites.

"I went kicking and screaming," Mark admitted. "I thought, *you're going to keep me in a city instead of in a cabin in the woods?* But...happy wife, happy life."

"It was clearly God," Sue said. "Why else would we have gone there at that time?"

"It was the time when mentions of God were being removed from the public," Mark recalled. "We started at the Washington Monument. As we waited in the line wrapped around the monument, we were able to read quotes from George Washington and it became apparent how much God was a part of his thinking and how much a part of our nation's foundation.

Next, we went to the Lincoln Memorial. I was walking up the steps and it was as if Abraham Lincoln was looking at us and asking us, "*What are you doing to my country?*"

"Inside the Lincoln Memorial, the name of God is found all over. When we looked to the left, we saw the Gettysburg Address on one wall and on the right was the second inaugural address."

The Gettysburg Address was particularly moving:

> "*Four score and seven years ago our fathers brought forth on this continent a new nation conceived in liberty and dedicated to the proposition that all men are created equal....*

> "*That this nation, under God, shall have a new birth of freedom and that government of the people, by the people, and for the people, shall not perish from the earth.*"

"These were powerful, moving words," Mark said. "The second inaugural address referred to God many, many times. This was not a church document but rather our nation's leader addressing America speaking at a public forum. We were moved by how much our nation had changed. Perhaps the fact that our three children were along with us on this our first visit to our nation's capital made it even more moving."

Matt, who was six years old at the time, decided to try sliding down the rail of the steps, Sue recalled. A guard came over to remind them to respect the site.

Tricia, Andy, and Matt in front of the Washington Monument.

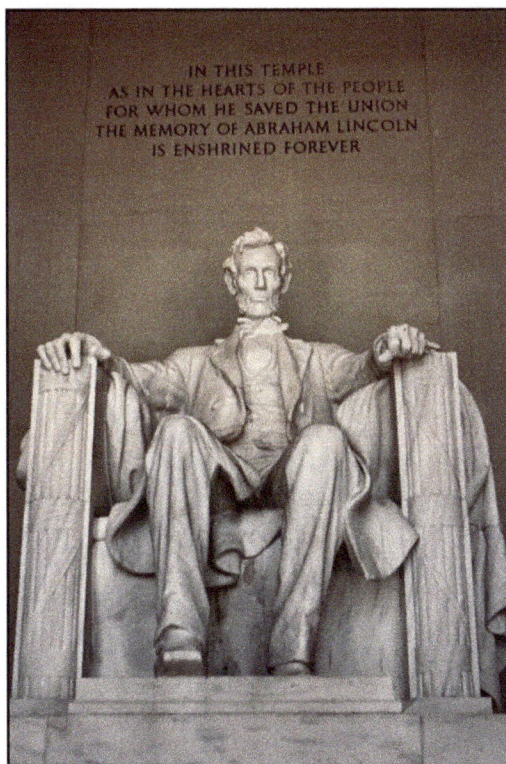

Abraham Lincoln statue, DC trip, 1989.

The family had been staying in Crystal City, Virginia, part of Arlington. "I called the hotel and extended our stay by four nights," Sue said. "We had planned to stay for two nights and ended up staying of six!

They visited other area sites. They were especially struck by the rendering over the door frame of the Capitol Congressional Chamber. The words, *In God We Trust*, can be seen from the gallery during a tour. They saw the Bill of Rights, visited part of the Smithsonian Institute, and the White House.

"The last thing we did before we left Washington was visit Arlington National Cemetery," Mark said. "We looked out over row after row of white grave stones and monuments of the many who had given their all for this nation."

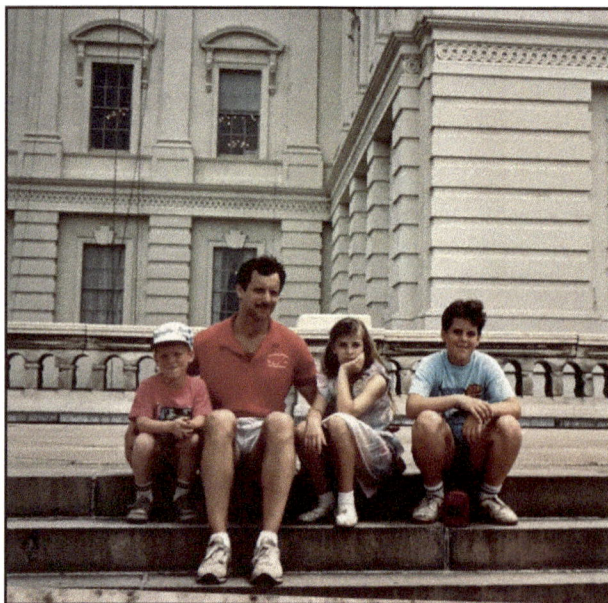

Matt, Mark, Tricia, and Andy on congressional building steps, DC trip, 1989.

Arlington National Cemetery, DC trip, 1989.

Mark, Sue, Matt (6),
Tricia (10), and Andy (11)
DC trip, 1989.

Mark and Sue
with Capitol,
DC trip, 1989.

Washington, DC trip, Mark, Sue, Andy, Tricia, and Matt, 1989.

Statue of Liberty. Mark, Sue, Andy, Tricia, and Matt, trip to New York City, 1989.

"We thought, wait a minute—look at all these people who died to give us our America," Sue said. "And we thought about what was happening to our country now.

"The trip made such an impression on us," Mark said. "What, morally and ethically, were we—our generation—doing to our country?" He was unable to get the thought he'd had at the Lincoln Memorial and at Arlington National Cemetery out of his head.

Also on his mind was the Social Security paper he'd written during his work on a PhD at UW–Madison in 1978, and the discussions on math and finance in his U–Rock math classes he taught.

"I knew our nation wasn't solvent going forward. The share of a family of four of the national debt was what we were selling houses for. The national debt crossed $1 trillion in 1982, and it was growing.

"Then there was the abortion question. We believe life begins at conception. Luke 1:41, 'When Elizabeth heard Mary's greeting, the baby leaped in her womb.'"

"I thought, *What are Mark and I doing personally to preserve our country?*" Sue said. "Is there something else we could do?"

"It was me, a math teacher, seeing in numbers what was happening in Washington with debt, the deficit, and Social Security," Mark said. "I had a genuine fear for our country—a genuine fear of financial collapse."

"We became worried about the future," Sue added.

They continued their vacation after the Arlington stop, traveling to New York City and seeing the Statue of Liberty. The family also visited Washington's home at Mount Vernon, Philadelphia and the Liberty Bell, area Civil War battlefields, and Niagara Falls.

"I found myself wondering, *Are we living up to our calling and our responsibility to our nation?*" Mark said.

"Besides my true calling as a New York City taxi driver," Mark added to lighten the conversation. "I should have been a taxi driver. I lost a hubcap. Everyone was honking their horns."

"The kids would say, 'Dad, honk the horn, and you'd honk the horn,'" Sue said. "Our horn actually gave out from overuse!"

They came home to ponder their calling.

He and Sue felt a need to do something. "We really felt it was God changing our lives again."

Little did they know what their future would hold!

*The Mark and Sue Neumann family story continues
with Book II, The Congressional Years.*